RVer's Guide
to Dump Stations

A comprehensive directory of
RV dump stations across the United States

Published by
Roundabout Publications
PO Box 19235
Lenexa, KS 66285

Phone
800-455-2207

Internet
www.RVdumps.com
www.RoadNotes.com
www.TravelBooksUSA.com

Please Note
Every effort has been made to make this book as complete and as accurate as possible. However, there may be mistakes both typographical and in content. Therefore, this text should be used as a general guide to dump stations in the United States. Although we regret any inconvenience caused by inaccurate information, the author and Roundabout Publications shall have neither liability nor responsibility to any person or entity with respect to any loss or damage caused, or alleged to be caused, directly or indirectly by the information contained in this book.

ISBN: 1-885464-13-4
Library of Congress Control Number: 2005931711

Contents

Introduction

This book is designed to help you easily locate RV dump stations across America. Understanding how to use it will aid you in your search.

Dump station locations are organized by state. Those easily accessed from Interstate highways are listed first, followed by those in other locations. Interstate highways are listed by their number from lowest to highest. For dump stations in other locations, each site is listed alphabetically by city or town name.

Interstate Highways

RV dump stations located along Interstate highways are presented in a chart (see the sample below). Depending on your direction of travel, you'll either read up the chart or read down the chart (see **Understanding Mile Markers and Exit Numbers** below). If you are traveling north or east, read up the chart. If you are traveling south or west, read down the chart.

Interstate No.

A brief description of the Interstate is provided here. This will tell you how long the Interstate is and the general direction of travel through the state.

Exit(mm)	Description
(66)	Welcome Center (wb)
44	**AL 59 / Loxley**
	Econ Family Center
	Love's Travel Stop
(1)	Welcome Center (eb)

Exit numbers are listed in bold type. The column next to the exit number shows the city, town, street, or other highways accessed from that exit. Beneath the exit name is a list of each site that has a dump station. Included are truck stops and travel centers, gas stations, city and county parks, and other sites.

Any location, such as a rest area or welcome center, that is located *along* an Interstate (not at an exit) is identified by its mile marker number surrounded by parentheses. Sometimes you will notice an (nb), (sb), (eb), or (wb) after the site name. This means that the facility is only accessed by northbound, southbound, eastbound, or westbound travelers (see **Abbreviations** below).

Other Locations
Dump stations not located along Interstate highways are listed in this section. Each site is listed alphabetically by city or town name.

City or Town	Description
Name	Description of dump station site

Understanding Mile Markers and Exit Numbers
Mile markers, or mileposts as they are also known, are the vertical green signs on the edge of highways placed at one-mile intervals. Mile marker numbering begins at the most southerly or westerly point in a state. For example, if you enter Colorado from New Mexico, mile markers will increase as you travel north through Colorado. Likewise if you were to enter Colorado from Utah, mile markers would increase as you travel east through Colorado. California is the only state that does not use mile markers. Instead they use a Post Mile system with numbering beginning and ending at county lines.

Interstate exit numbers are determined by one of two methods. The first, and most widely used, is based on the mile marker system. Using this method, the first exit number on an Interstate as you travel south to north or west to east is determined by its distance from the state line. For example, if an exit is located between mile markers 4 and 5, it is numbered as Exit 4. The next exit, if located at mile marker 8.7, would be numbered as Exit 8. Thus you would know that you must travel approximately 4 miles to reach the next exit. Using this method of exit numbering helps to determine the location and distance to a desired exit.

The second method of numbering Interstate exits is the consecutive numbering system, which means Interstate exit numbers begin at the most southerly or westerly point and increase consecutively as you travel north or east. Using this method, the first exit on an Interstate as you travel south to north or west to east is Exit 1. Each exit thereafter increases consecutively as Exit 2, Exit 3 and so on. Few states use this method.

As mentioned above, California does not use mile markers nor does it indicate exits with a number. This is changing, however. In January of 2002, California began erecting signs displaying exit numbers based on the mile marker system. Completion of this project is expected in 2008. The exit numbers and mile marker numbers used in this book are based on the new proposed numbers that California has assigned.

Abbreviations
Below is a list of abbreviations used in this book.

Abbreviation	Description
Blvd	Boulevard
CR	County Road
E	East
eb	Eastbound
FM	Farm to Market Road
Hwy	Highway
I	Interstate
N	North
nb	Northbound
NRA	National Recreation Area
Pkwy	Parkway
Rd	Road
S	South
sb	Southbound
US	U.S. Highway
W	West
wb	Westbound

Suggestions or Corrections

If you know of a dump station that is not listed in this book or a location that no longer provides this service, please visit our web site (www.rvdumps.com) and complete the "Suggestions/Corrections" form. Your comments are greatly appreciated and helpful to all RV dump station users.

Final Note

Please keep in mind that public dump stations are subject to closure for a number of reasons including state budget cuts and dump station abuse. See Appendix C for more information about dump station abuse.

Alabama

Below is a list of RV dump stations in Alabama. Listed first are those easily accessed from Interstate highways followed by those in other locations throughout the state.

Interstate 10

Interstate 10 runs east to west for 67 miles from the Florida state line to the Mississippi state line. Eastbound travelers should read up the chart. Westbound travelers read down the chart.

Exit(mm)	Description
(66)	Welcome Center (wb)
53	**CR 64**
	Oasis Travel Center
44	**AL 59 / Loxley**
	Econ Family Center
	Love's Travel Stop
22	**AL 163 / Dauphin Island Pkwy / Mobile**
	Shady Acre RV Park, no fee
	Comments: From exit go south on AL 163 to first light, turn on Old Military Rd, one block on the right, potable water available
(1)	Welcome Center (eb)

Interstate 20

Interstate 20 runs east to west for approximately 215 miles from the Georgia state line to the Mississippi state line. A portion of the highway from Birmingham to Mississippi is also I-59. Eastbound travelers should read up the chart. Westbound travelers read down the chart.

Exit(mm)	Description
(213)	Welcome Center (wb)
104	**McAshan Dr / Rock Mountain Lake**
	Flying J Travel Plaza
(85)	Rest Area
77	**Buttermilk Rd / to Cottondale**
	TA Travel Center

(39)	Rest Area (wb)
(38)	Rest Area (eb)
(.5)	Welcome Center (eb)

Interstate 59

Interstate 59 runs north to south for 242 miles from the Georgia state line to the Mississippi state line. A portion of the highway from Birmingham to Mississippi is also I-20. Northbound travelers should read up the chart. Southbound travelers read down the chart.

Exit(mm)	Description
(241)	Welcome Center (sb)
(168)	Rest Area (sb)
(165)	Rest Area (nb)
104	**McAshan Dr / Rock Mountain Lake**
	Flying J Travel Plaza
(85)	Rest Area
77	**Buttermilk Rd / to Cottondale**
	TA Travel Center
(39)	Rest Area (sb)
(38)	Rest Area (nb)
(.5)	Welcome Center (nb)

Interstate 65

Interstate 65 runs north to south for 367 miles from the Tennessee state line to Interstate 10. Northbound travelers should read up the chart. Southbound travelers read down the chart.

Exit(mm)	Description
(364)	Welcome Center (sb)
334	**AL 67 / Priceville / to Decatur**
	Pilot Travel Center
(302)	Rest Area
264	**41st Ave / Birmingham**
	Flying J Travel Plaza
(213)	Rest Area
(134)	Rest Area
(89)	Rest Area (sb)

(85)	Welcome Center (nb)
69	**AL 113 / to Flomaton**
	Conoco Minute Stop
19	**US 43 / to Satsuma**
	Pilot Travel Center

Interstate 85

Interstate 85 runs north to south for 80 miles from the Georgia state line to I-65 in Montgomery. Northbound travelers should read up the chart. Southbound travelers read down the chart.

Exit(mm)	Description
(78)	Welcome Center (sb)
(44)	Rest Area

Other Locations

City or Town	Description
Centre	Amoco on US 411
Dothan	Welcome Center on US 231 at Alabama/Florida state line, 12 miles south of Dothan, no charge
Eufaula	Rest area on US 431 about 5 miles south of town. Free.
Marion	Lakeview Park near the public golf course, $10
Florala	Rest area on US 331 about 10 miles north of Florala. Attendants keep this clean. Free.
Ozark	Inland Travel Stop on US 231 at AL 123. Easy access north or south bound. Dump site is on the west side of the building. Free
Ozark	Rest area on southbound side of US 231 about 5 miles south of town. 24-hour attendant, water hose at dump site. Free
Wetumpka	Fort Toulouse/Jackson Park campground west of US 231 on Fort Toulouse Rd
Woodville	Parnell Creek RV Park and Bed & Breakfast, 24 miles east of Huntsville off US 72 at Parnell Cir, $5 fee

Alaska

Below is a list of RV dump stations in Alaska.

Other Locations

City or Town	Description
Anchorage	Williams Express at Glenn Hwy and Muldoon Rd S
Dead Horse	NANA Oilfield Services Inc at end of Dalton Highway, go west 2.2 miles to the Time and Temp sign.
Eagle	Eagle Trading Company on Taylor Hwy at mile marker 161
Fairbanks	Alaska Chevron, 333 Illinois St, 907-452-3025, fee unknown
Fairbanks	Mike's University Chevron, 3245 College Rd, 907-479-7060, fee unknown
Fairbanks	Sourdough Fuel on Johansen Expy at Danby, no water, large area to get in and out, free
Fairbanks	Tanana Valley State Fairgrounds along College Rd, fee unknown
Fairbanks	Tesoro Truck Stop at Cushman and Van Horn streets
Fairbanks	Williams Express at 23rd and Cushman streets
Haines	Bigfoot Auto Service at 987 Haines Hwy
Haines	Delta Western gas station at 900 W Main St
Juneau	Mendenhall Lake Campground (US Forest Service) about 13 miles northwest of Juneau off AK 7
Ketchikan	Ketchikan Public Works at 3291 Tongass Ave, 2 blocks north of ferry terminal, no charge
Palmer	Chevron gas station at intersection of Glenn Hwy and Palmer-Wasilla Rd, $2 or free with fuel purchase.
Soldotna	Fred Meyer, 43843 Sterling Hwy. Parking lot striped for RVs on north side. Overnighters welcome.
Tok	Tesoro Northern Energy Corp on Alaska Hwy at mile marker 1314
Tok	Young's Chevron at Alaska Hwy and Glenn Hwy
Valdez	Tesoro at Meals Ave and Eagen Ave
Wasilla	Chevron gas station on Parks Hwy next to Wells Fargo Bank, east end of town, free

Arizona

Below is a list of RV dump stations in Arizona. Listed first are those easily accessed from Interstate highways followed by those in other locations throughout the state.

Interstate 8

Interstate 8 runs east to west for about 178 miles from Interstate 10 to the California state line. Eastbound travelers should read up the chart. Westbound travelers read down the chart.

Exit(mm)	Description
119	**Butterfield Trail / to Gila Bend**
	Holt's Shell Truck Stop
115	**AZ 85 / to Gila Bend**
	Love's Travel Stop
	McDonalds
	Subway
	Texaco

Interstate 10

Interstate 10 runs east to west for about 391 miles from the New Mexico state line to the California state line. Eastbound travelers should read up the chart. Westbound travelers read down the chart.

Exit(mm)	Description
340	**AZ 186 / to Willcox**
	Rip Griffin Travel Center
302	**AZ 90 S**
	Gas City Truck Stop
268	**Craycroft Rd**
	Mr T's Self Serve
	Comments: Dump is to the back on the west end. It is not well maintained
	Triple T Truck Stop
264	**Irvington Rd / Tucson**
	Camping World / Beaudry RV Park; west on Irvington Rd; Beaudry's RV Park is on left. Take a left at the "T" in the road

and on the right in cul-de-sac is dump station and fresh water. Free

254	**Prince Rd**
	Arizona Roadrunner RV Service Center, 4324 N Flowing Wells Rd, free
	Comments: From exit travel east to third traffic light, turn left (north) on Flowing Wells Rd and go north about one mile.
208	**Sunshine Blvd / to Eloy**
	Flying J Travel Plaza
	Pilot Travel Center
203	**Toltec Rd / to Eloy**
	TA Travel Center
200	**Sunland Gin Rd / to Arizona City**
	Love's Travel Stop
137	**67th Ave**
	Flying J Travel Plaza
114	**Miller Rd / to Buckeye**
	Love's Travel Stop
94	**411th Ave / Tonopah**
	El Dorado Hot Springs, 41225 Indian School Rd
	Comments: Dump is free with purchase of a hot mineral water soak, located 1/4 mile west of 411th Ave
45	**Vicksburg Rd**
	Tomahawk Auto & Truck Plaza, $5 fee
1	**Juneau Ave / Ehrenberg**
	Flying J Travel Plaza, 14380 S Frontage Rd, 520-923-9600. Dump is on the right side of the building.

Interstate 17

Interstate 17 runs north to south for about 147 miles from I-40 in Flagstaff to I-10 in Phoenix. Northbound travelers should read up the chart. Southbound travelers read down the chart.

Exit(mm)	Description
287	**AZ 260 / Finnie Flats Rd / Camp Verde**
	Shell gas station just off the Interstate next to McDonald's, $5
205	**W Glendale Ave / Phoenix**
	Grand Service Station on N 35th Ave, one mile west of exit, $5

Interstate 40

Interstate 40 runs east to west for 360 miles from the New Mexico state line to the California state line. Eastbound travelers should read up the chart. Westbound travelers read down the chart.

Exit(mm)	Description
255	**to I-40 Bus / Winslow** Flying J Travel Plaza
253	**N Park Dr / Winslow** Pilot Travel Center
201	**Country Club Dr / US 89 / to Flagstaff** Unocal 76 at 3686 E Route 66 ($8 or free with fuel purchase)
198	**Butler Ave / to Flagstaff** Conoco at 2300 E Butler (free)
59	**CR 259 / DW Ranch Rd** Love's Travel Stop
53	**AZ 66 / Andy Devine Ave / to Kingman** Flying J Travel Plaza
48	**US 93 / W Beale St / Kingman** Mobile service station on Beale St (US 93) at Joyce St. Dump is on the north side of gas station, large area that can handle big rigs. Free

Other Locations

City or Town	Description
Apache Junction	RV 101 Parts & Service, 10918 E Apache Trail, 480-984-7283, $5 fee. Open 24 hours, deposit fee in drop box after business hours.
Cottonwood	Giant Service Station at junction of Hwy 89A and AZ 260
Cottonwood	Verde Valley Fairgrounds at S 12th St and Hwy 89A
Flagstaff	Giant Service Station at 1205 S Milton (free)
Gila Bend	Minute Mart at 942 E AZ 85
Heber	Public dump station near Woods Canyon Lake in Sitgreaves National Forest, $6. The dump station is about 25 miles west of town and four miles north of AZ 260 via FSR 300 and FSR 105.
Lake Havasu City	Arco AM-PM gas station, 311 Lake Havasu Ave N, 928-453-3832. One block east of AZ 95 at Palo Verde Blvd S, free.

Mesa	Apache Sands Car Care Center at 7602 E Apache Trail, $5 fee
Mesa	Chevron station on Ellsworth Rd about 3 miles north of Superstition Fwy (US 60), no charge
Mesa	Desert RV Parts & Service Center at 9736 E Apache Trail, $4-5 fee
Morenci	Conoco Gas/Convenience store just off US 191, free, watch for sign, water available
Payson	Giant Gas Station at 701 E Highway 260
Payson	Ponderosa Campground in Tonto National Forest on AZ 260, 928-474-7900, free if staying at this campground or other USFS campgrounds (save your receipt as proof).
Phoenix	Superpumper on N Cave Creek Rd just north of Bell Rd on east side, about 2 miles south of AZ 101 Exit 28
Prescott	City wastewater treatment plant on Sundog Ranch Rd off AZ 89 about two miles north of town, open 7 days a week, closes earlier on weekends and holidays, no charge
Prescott Valley	Many Trails RV on AZ 69, 928-775-5770, $3
Roosevelt	Cholla Bay Recreation Site (national forest campground) on AZ 188 at milepost 249, north of Roosevelt, no charge
Safford	The city of Safford provides a free dump station but no drinking water at the city waste disposal plant located on N 8th Ave near the Gila River. The site is designed for septic tanker trucks with outlets at the rear of the truck, so the reach is a little long for RV's with side outlets.
Scottsdale	Public dump station in WestWorld equestrian center. From AZ 101 Loop, take the Frank Lloyd Wright Blvd exit and follow signs. $3 fee. Pay at RV office before dumping.
Sierra Vista	Gas City near junction of AZ 90 and AZ 92 next to Ford dealership. Free
Surprise	Orangewood RV Center, 11449 W Bell Rd, 623-974-3000, free, no water. Dump stations are located on the north and south side of propane tank.
Surprise	Van's RV-Trailer Company, 11565 W Bell Rd

Arkansas

Below is a list of RV dump stations in Arkansas. Listed first are those easily accessed from Interstate highways followed by those in other locations throughout the state.

Interstate 30

Interstate 30 runs east to west from Interstate 40 in North Little Rock to the Texas state line. The highway is approximately 143 miles long. Eastbound travelers should read up the chart. Westbound travelers read down the chart.

Exit(mm)	Description
46	**AR 19 / Prescott**
	Love's Travel Stop
44	**AR 24 / Prescott**
	Rip Griffin Travel Center
7	**AR 108 / Mandeville**
	Flying J Travel Plaza

Interstate 40

Interstate 40 is about 285 miles long. It runs east to west from the Tennessee state line to the Oklahoma state line. Eastbound travelers should read up the chart. Westbound travelers read down the chart.

Exit(mm)	Description
280	**Club Rd / Southland Dr**
	Flying J Travel Plaza
	Pilot Travel Center
278	**AR 77 / 7th St / Missouri St**
	Flash Market
233	**AR 261 / Palestine**
	Love's Travel Stop
193	**US 63 / AR 11 / to Hazen**
	T Ricks RV Park, 3001 Hwy 11N, 870-255-4914, $4
150	**Military Dr / Charles H Boyer Dr**
	Burns Park (city park), $5 fee. Dump is located in the campground south of the exit; follow signs to campground.

84	US 64 / AR 331 / Russellville
	Flying J Travel Plaza
	Pilot Travel Center
55	US 64 / AR 109 / Clarksville
	Highway 109 Truck Plaza

Interstate 55

Interstate 55 runs north to south for 72 miles from the Missouri state line to the Tennessee state line. A small stretch of I-55 in West Memphis is also I-40. Northbound travelers should read up the chart. Southbound travelers read down the chart.

Exit(mm)	Description
63	US 61 / to Blytheville
	Phoenix Truck Plaza
278	AR 77 / 7th St / Missouri St
	Flash Market
4	King Dr / Southland Dr
	Flying J Travel Plaza
	Pilot Travel Center

Interstate 530

Interstate 530 is about 46 miles long. It runs north to south from Little Rock to Pine Bluff. Northbound travelers should read up the chart. Southbound travelers read down the chart.

Exit(mm)	Description
34	US 270
	Big Red Travel Plaza

Interstate 540

Interstate 540 runs north to south for approximately 90 miles from Bentonville to Fort Smith. Northbound travelers should read up the chart. Southbound travelers read down the chart.

Exit(mm)	Description
29	Dollard Rd
	Silver Bridge Auto & Truck Plaza

Other Locations

City or Town	Description
Hope	Fair Park (city park) off AR 174 at Park Dr
Horseshoe Bend	Box Hound Marina, 2 miles southeast of town via AR 289 and Tri-Lakes Dr. Also has an RV park, cabin rentals, and boat rentals.
Pine Bluff	Hestand Stadium (district fairgrounds) at 420 N Blake St
Pine Bluff	Pine Bluff Convention Center at 500 E 8th Ave
Pine Bluff	Saracen Trace RV Park (city park) on US 65 Business (Martha Mitchell Expressway)
Pocahontas	Black River City Park on US 67 just south of town
Siloam Springs	Super 8 Motel at 1800 US 412W, $5 fee. Also has a 37 unit RV park with full hookups.

California

Below is a list of RV dump stations in California. Listed first are those easily accessed from Interstate highways followed by those in other locations throughout the state.

Interstate 5

Interstate 5 runs north to south for approximately 797 miles from the Oregon state line to the Mexico border. Northbound travelers should read up the chart. Southbound travelers read down the chart.

Exit(mm)	Description
681b	**Market St / CA 273 / Southbound exit only**
	Exxon service station at southwest corner of N Market St and Caterpillar Rd
	Comments: Northbound travelers use Exit 680 (CA 299 / Lake Blvd) and go west to N Market St and then north to Caterpillar Rd.
667	**Deschutes Road / Factory Outlets Drive**
	Shell Service Station directly across from Prime Outlets
630	**South Ave / Corning**
	TA Travel Center
(608)	Willows Rest Area
537	**Main St / CA 113 S / Woodland**
	Bill Lowe's Tires, 801 East St, 530-666-1088, $10. From exit go west on Main St to East St and turn left (south).
	Comments: Dump available only during business hours, call. Must leave driver's license, pay fee and get key to unlock the lock on the dump hole lid. Dump is located on the east side of property along the tree line. Note: tree limbs are low.
	Yolo County Fairgrounds, 1125 East St, 530-662-5393, free
485	**CA 12 / to Lodi**
	Flying J Travel Plaza
(445)	Westley Rest Area
407	**CA 33 / Santa Nella Village**
	TA Travel Center
257	**CA 58 / to Buttonwillow**
	TA Travel Center

219	**Laval Rd**
	Petro Stopping Center
	TA Travel Center
205	**Frazier Park**
	Flying J Travel Plaza
(204)	Tejon Pass Rest Area
167	**Lyons Ave / Pico Canyon Rd**
	Camping World
152	**Lankershim Blvd / Sun Valley**
	BenchMark RV, $25
110	**Harbor Blvd / Ball Rd / Anaheim**
	Anaheim Resort RV Park, 200 W Midway Dr, 714-774-3860. From exit follow Ball Rd east to Anaheim Blvd and then south to Midway Dr, turn right (west). A fee is charged.
96	**Sand Canyon Ave / Irvine**
	El Toro RV Service Center, $8
	McMahon RV at 6441 Burt Rd #10
91	**El Toro Rd / Lake Forest**
	Chevron gas station, $5; dump station is located next to the propane tanks on south end of lot.
79	**CA 1 / Pacific Coast Hwy / Camino Las Ramblas**
	Doheny State Beach, must pay day-use fee
(60)	Aliso Creek Rest Area
54c	**Oceanside Harbor Dr / Oceanside**
	Oceanside Harbor Boat Ramp, free
	Comments: On west side of harbor, circle around south side to approach, across from boat launch area, two stations in the lane
41b	**Encinitas Blvd**
	San Elijo State Beach, $4 fee
	Comments: From exit, follow Encinitas Blvd west to Pacific Coast Hwy 101, turn south and go approximately two miles to state beach
22	**Clairmont Dr / Mission Bay Dr / San Diego**
	Mission Bay Information Center on E Mission Bay Dr, free
21	**Sea World Dr / San Diego**
	South Shores Boat Launch
	Comments: Follow Sea World Dr to South Shores Boat Launch just before Sea World on right (north side of road)

Interstate 8

Interstate 8 runs east to west for 172 miles from the Arizona state line to Sunset Cliffs Blvd in San Diego. Eastbound travelers should read up the chart. Westbound travelers read down the chart.

Exit(mm)	Description
166	**CA 186 / Andrade Rd**
	Sleepy Hollow RV Park, 369 Andrade Rd, 760-572-5101, $5. Located 1.25 miles south of exit.
164	**Sidewinder Rd**
	Shell service station, 611 Sidewinder Rd, 760-572-2053. Fee varies.
115	**CA 86 / El Centro**
	Imperial 8 Travel Center
(108)	Sunbeam Rest Area
51	**Buckman Springs Rd**
	Buckman Springs Rest Area
20	**Greenfield Dr / El Cajon**
	Vacationer RV Resort, 1581 E Main St, 619-442-0904, $10

Interstate 10

Interstate 10 runs east to west for approximately 244 miles from the Arizona state line to CA 1 in Santa Monica. Eastbound travelers should read up the chart. Westbound travelers read down the chart.

Exit(mm)	Description
222	**Wiley's Well Rd**
	Wiley's Well Rest Area
146	**Dillon Rd**
	Love's Travel Stop
	TA Travel Center
130	**Ramon Rd / Thousand Palms**
	Flying J Travel Plaza, free with fuel purchase, $5 without
	Comments: Dump station is in the automobile bay on the far right lane, across an island from the truck bay and propane fill. It is very difficult access for large vehicles. The store is directly in front of the automobile bays and there is little turn room to maneuver. Suggest checking it out before entering.

104	**Apache Trail / Cabazon** Dump station is at the Shell gas station owned by Casino Morongo, 49750 Seminole Dr, 800-252-4499, $5 fee, free overnight parking allowed in casino parking lot
76	**California St / Redlands** Mission RV Park, 26397 Redlands Blvd, 909-796-7570, south of exit, $8 fee
50	**Mountain Ave / Ontario** Arrow Trailer Supply on W Holt Blvd, 909-986-3737, $3 fee, honor system for 24-hour operation. *Comments*: Arrow Trailer Supply is two miles south of exit. Dump station is on a side street, east side of store, just in from the curb. Green's Trailer Supply, 120 N Benson Ave, 909-983-1311, $2. Located one block north of Holt Blvd. Open during business hours. *Comments*: Green's Trailer Supply is two miles south of exit.
45	**N Garey Ave / Pomona (westbound exit only)** KOA next to Fairplex, 2200 N White Ave, $10 *Comments:* From exit go north one mile to Arrow Hwy; west to White Ave; south to KOA.
45a	**White Ave / Pomona (eastbound exit only)** KOA next to Fairplex, 2200 N White Ave, $10 *Comments:* From exit go north 1.3 miles to KOA
44	**Dudley St / Fairplex Dr (westbound travelers)** East Shore RV Park, 1440 Camper View Rd, $5 *Comments:* From exit go north on Fairplex Dr to Via Verde; west to Camper View Rd; north to RV park.
43	**Fairplex Dr / La Verne (eastbound travelers)** East Shore RV Park, 1440 Camper View Rd, $5 *Comments:* From exit go north on Fairplex Dr to Via Verde; west to Camper View Rd; north to RV park.

Interstate 15

Interstate 15 runs north to south for about 292 miles from the Nevada state line to San Diego. Northbound travelers should read up the chart. Southbound travelers read down the chart.

Exit(mm)	Description
246	**CA 127 / Kelbaker Rd / Baker**
	Ultra Gas Station on Baker Blvd, $5
178	**Lenwood Rd**
	Flying J Travel Plaza, 2611 Fisher Blvd
	Rip Griffin Travel Center
141	**Joshua St / US 395 / Hesperia**
	Newton's Outpost Cafe & Truck N Travel, $5. Dump station is located at the truck wash/lube and brake stations directly facing I-15. Lots of parking for boondocking.
122	**Glen Helen Pkwy**
	Glen Helen Regional Park
	Comments: You must go to the main entrance to pay the $5 fee. The attendant will call a ranger to unlock the dump station, if necessary, and provide you with directions.
58	**CA 79 S / Front St**
	Pechanga Casino RV Park, $6 fee
	Comments: From I-15 exit proceed east to Pechanga Pkwy, turn right and proceed to casino on right. Stop at office and pay fee before dumping.
	Temecula Valley RV service center on Front St, $5

Interstate 80

Interstate 80 runs east to west for 208 miles from the Nevada state line to 7th Street in San Francisco. Eastbound travelers should read up the chart. Westbound travelers read down the chart.

Exit(mm)	Description
109	**Sierra College Blvd / Loomis**
	Loomis RV Park, 3945 Taylor Rd
	Comments: North on Sierra College Blvd to Taylor Rd and turn right, $7 fee

105a	**Atlantic St / Eureka Rd / Roseville**
	Chevron station at Rocky Ridge Dr and Eureka Rd. $4 fee or free with propane or fuel purchase.
94a	**Watt Ave / Auburn Blvd / Sacramento**
	Arco Gas Station
	Comments: Take Watt Ave exit off I-80 or Capital City Freeway (Bus I-80) and go south across Auburn Blvd, entrance on right, $3.50 fee
85	**W El Camino Ave**
	Sacramento 49er Travel Plaza, 2828 El Centro Rd, 916-927-4774, $5 unless you purchase 12 or more gallons of fuel. *Comments*: Dump station is located to the right side of the gas station along the property edge. Can be a confusing area to enter. Call first for directions on how to enter to find the dump station.
75	**Mace Blvd / Davis**
	Chevron service station, 4475 Chiles Rd, 530-756-4250, free. Westbound travelers turn left at exit and then right onto Chiles Rd. Eastbound travelers should stay in right lane when exiting; turn right at light and station is immediately on your right. *Comments*: Enter the station via the entrance on the left (west) side of the property. Drive around behind the station to the right (east) side of the property. RV dump is located on very right (east) edge of property under trees. Note: tree limbs are low. Easy entrance and exit with large RVs.
63	**Dixon Ave / West A St / Dixon**
	Arco Gas Station, free. Dump station is privately located between two hedges on the northwest side of the gas station.
41	**Suisun Valley Rd**
	Camping World

Interstate 880

Interstate 880 in California runs north to south for about 46 miles from I-80 in Oakland to I-280 in San Jose. Northbound travelers should read up the chart. Southbound travelers read down the chart.

Exit(mm)	Description
16	**Stevenson Blvd**
	Shell Service Station, 510-656-1704, $8 or free with $50 fill-up. Not recommended for big rigs due to tight access to dump.

15   Durham Rd / Auto Mall Pkwy
Automall RV & Boat Storage, 42335 Boscell Rd, $10; located west of exit.

Other Locations

City or Town	Description
Arcata	From US 101, take the Valley West/Giuntoli Ln exit, north end of town. Turn east and go one block. Gas station is on southwest corner of Giuntoli Ln at first stop sign. Dump is on Valley West side of station near the car wash. $2 fee. A California welcome center is on other side of freeway at this exit.
Baker	Tecopa Hot Springs County Park, 55 miles north of Baker via CA 127, in the center of Tecopa Hot Springs on west side of road
Bakersfield	Bakersfield Palms RV Park, $5. From CA 99 go east six miles on CA 58 to Fairfax Road; north 1/2 mile to RV park.
Bakersfield	Camping World off Hwy 99 at Panama Ln. Dump is at east end of store by loading ramp.
Bakersfield	Flying J Travel Plaza on CA 99 at Merced Ave exit
Big Sur	Public dump station in Pfeiffer Big Sur State Park, $8 fee. Site is east of CA 1 in the bottom of Big Sur Valley at the campground.
Boron	Rest area on CA 58 about 5 miles west of Boron between mile markers 188 and 189
Brawley	Rest area on CA 111, 6 miles north of town, very clean and well maintained
Calistoga	Napa County Fairgrounds at 1435 Oak St, $2 fee
Cameron Park	Shell service station, 3405 Coach Ln, 530-677-9129. Take the Cameron Park Dr exit from US 50. $3 with 8 gallon fuel purchase or $5 without. Plenty of space to maneuver.
Chino	Park and Ride parking lot at Chino Valley Freeway (CA 71) and Chino Ave. Not accessible during weekdays because of full parking lot. Free
Chowchilla	Arena Mobile Home Park, 203 S Chowchilla Blvd, 559-665-1752, $10
Fortuna	Shell gas station on Fortuna Blvd behind station in front of Safeway store, free
Garden Grove	Elks Lodge at corner of Trask Ave and Newhope St. Also has 19 RV sites with electricity and water (members only).

	Accessed from the Garden Grove Freeway (CA 22) at Euclid St Exit. Dump is free to Elks members; $5 donation requested for non-members.
Gilroy	The Garlic Farm Center at US 101 and Monterey Rd
Grass Valley	Nevada County Fairgrounds near junction of CA 20 and CA 49. Follow fairground signs to gate #4. Unit is locked, call 530-273-6217 for times available or when attendant is on duty. $5 fee.
Grass Valley	Sierra Auto Center & U-Haul, $7. From Golden Center Freeway take the Brunswick Rd exit and go west to the old Nevada City Hwy. Turn south to Dorsey Dr. Continue past the signal light - on the right.
Hemet	Hemet Trailer Supply at 1371 W Acacia Ave (south of CA 74 and S Hamilton Ave intersection), $2 fee, dump open 24 hours, in a large parking area, always clean and functional
Hollister	Casa de Fruita on CA 152 near Hollister
Holtville	The chamber of commerce has built and maintains a dump station in the 400 block of Holt Ave. There is no charge but donations are accepted. There is also fresh water available for filling up your fresh water tank.
Huntington Beach	Bolsa Chica State Beach, $6 fee to get into beach parking area where dump is located. Camping is also available.
Indio	Texaco Truck Stop at 84425 Indio Blvd (CA 111)
Indio	Wastewater Treatment Plant at 45500 Van Buren St
Jackson	Bear River Lake Resort, 40800 Hwy 88, 209-295-4868, $7. The resort campground is located 42 miles east of Jackson on CA 88. Open April thru October.
Joshua Tree	Joshua Tree Lake RV & Campground, 2601 Sunfair Rd, 760-366-1213, $4. Located four miles east of Park Blvd and five miles north on Sunfair Rd.
Lancaster	Dump is at the City of Lancaster National Soccer Field on Avenue L at 30th St E, north side of park, nice level pull through and non-potable water for flushing tanks, no fee. The dump station is on the north side of the east parking lot (not easy to find in this large facility). Washdown water furnished, but no drinking water. Closed 10pm to 6am.
Lancaster	Youngs RV Center, 661-942-8447, Free. Located immediately off of CA 14 at Avenue I.
Lemon Grove	Gas Stop at 7988 Broadway, $5 fee. Gas Stop is about 1/2 mile south of CA 94 Exit 8.

Manteca	Manteca Trailer & Motorhome Inc, 1990 E Yosemite (CA 120), 209-239-1267, free
Markleeville	Indian Creek Campground (BLM) on Airport Rd about 4 miles off CA 89. Gate to dump station is often closed - must get manager to open.
Menifee	Wilderness Lakes Resort, 30605 Briggs Rd, 951-672-4831, $5 fee. From Riverside take I-215 south. Two miles past Sun City, take the Newport Rd exit and go left 1.9 miles. Turn right at Briggs Rd and go .7 miles to entrance. Do not enter in store parking lot, proceed to second entrance.
Modesto	Ward's RV Storage, 141 E Orangeburg Ave, $2
Mojave	Red Rock Canyon State Park, free, 25 miles northeast of town on CA 14, free if camping, $3 fee if not
Monterey	Monterey County Park at Laguna Seca Raceway about 3 miles east of Monterey on the north side of CA 68 ($6 fee). The dump is in the campground at the top of a very steep (12%) half-mile grade.
Morgan Hill	Parkway Lakes RV Park, 100 Ogier Ave, 408-779-0244, $12. Take the Bailey exit off US 101 and go west to Monterey Hwy. Go south two miles, campground is on left.
Newhall	Mobil gas station on San Fernando Rd, north of CA 14, $8
Niland	City park on west side of CA 111 near Main St, no fee
Novato	Novato RV Park, 1530 Armstrong Ave, 415-897-1271, $5 fee. From US 101, take the San Marin Dr/Atherton Ave exit. Located about 25 miles north of the Golden Gate Bridge. Available to public during business hours Mon-Sun.
Oakdale	Tiger Express Chevron at 977 S Yosemite Blvd, $5 fee
Old Station	US Forest Service Information Station near junction of CA 44 and CA 89. Not marked by roadway but easy to find; directly behind information station. $5 requested donation.
Olema	Olema Ranch Campground, 10155 State Hwy 1, 800-655-2267, $10. Dump is near the propane. Pay first at the campground general store. Nice place to camp, too.
Oxnard	McGrath State Beach on Harbor Blvd between Ventura and Oxnard, $8
Petaluma	76 gas station off US 101 at Petaluma Blvd N, $5.50. The dump is at the rear of the gas station.
Redwood City	Trailer Villa RV Park, 3401E Bayshore Rd, 650-366-7880, $5
Ridgecrest	Desert Empire Fairgrounds. There is a small RV park at the south end of the fairgrounds. The free dump site is just

	north of the RV park. Lots of room to negotiate any size rig.
Ridgecrest	Public dump station at the Coso Junction rest stop east of US 395 about 40 miles north of Ridgecrest. The dump gets full by Sunday afternoons. No fee.
Ripon	Flying J Travel Plaza on CA 99 at Jack Tone Rd exit
Ripon	Love's Travel Stop on CA 99 at Jack Tone Rd exit
Rosamond	Chevron station on Rosamond Blvd, no fee. From CA 14, take the Rosamond Blvd exit and travel east 1/2 mile to Chevron station at corner; turn right and right again into last drive entering station; dump is in plain view next to phone booth and air pump.
Salinas	Chevron station off US 101 at Laurel St exit, $5 for free with fill-up
Salyer	Rest Area on CA 299
San Jose	Arnone's RV Rentals, 186 San Jose Ave, $10. From Highway 87 take the Curtner Ave exit and go east to Little Orchard; north to San Jose Ave; right to Arnone's RV Rentals.
San Jose	Family RV dealership, 2828 Monterey Rd, 408-365-1991, $20 fee, Mon-Sat 8am to 4pm. From US 101 use Tully Rd exit, west to Monterey Rd (CA 82), south to dealership.
San Lucas	Ultramar Beacon Truck Stop at US 101 and Wildhorse Rd between San Lucas and King City
San Luis Obispo	Shell gas station on Los Osos Valley Rd just west of US 101, free with fill-up
Santa Barbara	Cachuma Lake Recreation Area (county park) on CA 154 about 20 miles northwest of town, 805-686-5054, $6
Santa Barbara	Marborg Industries, 136 N Quarantina, 800-798-1852, free. From US 101 take the Milpas St exit and travel north to Yanonali St and turn west. Go 2 blocks and then left into sanitation company. Easy in and out - no backing up.
Santa Cruz	Steve's Unocal 76 at CA 1 and Soquel Dr; $9 with purchase of fuel or LP gas
Santa Rosa	Rotten Robbie's gas station off US 101 at Todd Rd, 55 E Todd Rd, 707-584-9610, $10 or free with $10 merchandise purchase
Santa Rosa	Rosa Vista Trailer Park, 1885 Santa Rosa Ave, 707-544-6977, $5, no dumping after 8pm
Santee	Santee Lakes Recreation Preserve (municipal park), 9010 Carlton Oaks Dr, 619-596-3141. $10 fee. Camping also available.

Simi Valley	Simi RV Wash & Service Center near Costco off the CA 118 freeway. Easily accessed and a large fuel station for large RVs. Free
Simi Valley	Union 76 station, two blocks south of CA 118 on corner of Sycamore Dr and Los Angeles Ave, $10
Sonoma	Shell service station on Broadway St one block south of town square. Dump is on left side of station. Plenty of room to get in and out. $10
Tipton	Rest Area on CA 99, north of town, no fee, good clean water
Tulelake	Public dump station across from True Hardware off CA 139 at Modoc Ave and D St, no charge
Turlock	Chevron gas station off CA 99 at the Los Banos/Lander Ave exit, fee unknown
Ukiah	Chevron station just off US 101 on E Perkins St, free
Valley Springs	Public dump stations in campgrounds at New Hogan Lake (Corps of Engineers) about 1.5 miles southeast of Valley Springs via CA 26 and Hogan Dam Rd. Open year-round. $6
Victorville	Mojave Narrows Regional Park (county park), 18000 Yates Rd, 760-245-2226, $3 fee. Can be reached from I-15 exit 147 (Bear Valley Rd) by traveling east 4 miles and then north on Ridge Crest Rd.
Watsonville	Pinto Lake Park (city park), 451 Green Valley Rd, 831-722-8129, $3 fee. From CA 1, take Green Valley Road exit and go thru 6 lights, last crossroad is Airport Blvd, go 1/2 mile and turn left
Willits	KOA, 1600 Hwy 20, 707-459-6179, $10
Yountville	Veterans Home of California - Yountville at CA 29 and California Dr. Check at guard station, then a short drive to the RV park. Free
Yucca Valley	Desert Sky Motel, 55492 29 Palms Hwy (CA 62)
Yucca Valley	Black Rock Campground in Joshua Tree National Park, donation requested. From CA 62 in town, follow Joshua Ln to its end and turn right for one block and then south to campground. N 34° 4.452' W 116° 23.253'

Colorado

Below is a list of RV dump stations in Colorado. Listed first are those easily accessed from Interstate highways followed by those in other locations throughout the state.

Interstate 25

Interstate 25 runs north to south for about 300 miles from the Wyoming state line to the New Mexico state line. Northbound travelers should read up the chart. Southbound travelers read down the chart.

Exit(mm)	Description
269b	**CO 14 / E Mulberry St / Fort Collins** Fort Collins CoOp, no fee *Comments*: CoOp is on NW Service Road, just north of CO 14. Dump station is free but the business appreciates you buying fuel or other items if you use dump. Phillips 66 gas station, $2 or free with fill-up, west of exit on south side of CO 14
184	**Meadows Parkway / US 85** Town of Castle Rock Service Center, free *Comments*: From exit, go west to Santa Fe Dr and turn south (left), follow to Justice Way and turn east (left). Watch for one story brick building on right, go thru gate, dump is on right, open Mon-Fri 8am to 5pm
161	**CO 105 / Woodmoor Dr / Monument** Colorado Heights Campground east side of I-25 on Monument Hill Rd, 8am to 8pm, $5 Lake of the Rockies Campground, 99 Mitchell Ave, 719-481-4227, 8am to 8pm, $5. From exit go west on 2nd St; cross railroad tracks and turn left on Mitchell Ave.
139	**US 24 Bypass / Colorado Springs** Pikes Peak Traveland, 719-596-2716, $8. From exit go east to Academy Blvd. Go north on Academy Blvd to Platte Ave and then east one mile. Dump station available during business hours only.

Interstate 70

Interstate 70 runs east to west for 447 miles from the Kansas state line to the Utah state line. Eastbound travelers should read up the chart. Westbound travelers read down the chart.

Exit(mm)	Description
(437)	Welcome Center (wb)
405	**CO 59 / Seibert**
	Shady Grove Campground, 306 Colorado Ave, 970-664-2218, $5 fee
285	**Airport Blvd**
	Flying J Travel Plaza
163	**Edwards / to US 6**
	Rest Area
90	**CO 13 / Rifle**
	Rest Area
	Comments: From exit, go north and follow rest area signs. Dump is located on the right as you exit the rest area.
19	**CO 340 / Fruita**
	Welcome Center

Interstate 76

Interstate 76 runs east to west from the Nebraska state line to I-70 in Denver. It is about 184 miles long. Eastbound travelers should read up the chart. Westbound travelers read down the chart.

Exit(mm)	Description
180	**US 385 / Julesburg**
	Welcome Center
125	**US 6 / Sterling**
	Rest Area
22	**E 152nd Ave / E Bromley Ln / Brighton**
	Co-op at 55 W Bromley Ln, $5. From exit travel west about 4 miles to Co-op.

Interstate 225

Interstate 225 in Colorado is 12 miles long. It primarily runs north to south, connecting I-70 Exit 282 with I-25 Exit 200.

Exit(mm)	Description
4	CO 83 / Parker Rd / Aurora
	Cherry Creek State Park, $5

Other Locations

City or Town	Description
Antonito	Conoco gas station on US 285 in town, $4 fee.
Bayfield	Bayfield City Park on US 160. Dump station is just south of restrooms in the park. Free
Buena Vista	Snowy Peaks RV Park on US 24, north end of town, $7 fee if not camping
Buena Vista	KOA campground on US 285 about one mile east of US 24 and US 285 junction, $10 fee
Colorado Springs	Pike's Peak Traveland, 4815 E Platte Ave, 800-458-9622 or 719-596-2716, $8 fee. Dump station is in the gated area to the far side of the repair garage; fee can be paid at sales desk.
Cortez	City park 1/2 block north of US 160 just west of Chamber of Commerce visitor center, no fee for dumping, 25 cents for about 60 gallons of water (controlled by timer)
Del Norte	A public dump station is at 1st and Spruce streets
Delta	Delta Chamber of Commerce on 3rd St between Main and Palmer. Turn west off Main St onto 3rd St, go 3/4 block, enter parking lot on left, dump is at end of lot. Free.
Durango	Santa Rita Park (Gateway Park) on US 160/550 about one mile south of Durango & Silverton Narrow Gauge Railroad depot, city park, no fee
Evans	Evans C-Store at 665 US 85 in Evans
Frisco	Breckenridge Sanitation Plant next to the Blue River Inlet on Dillon Reservoir about 3 miles east of Frisco via CO 9 ($2 fee)
Granby	Mega Matt Conoco at 308 W Agate Ave
Greeley	Missile Site Park, 10611 Spur 257, 970-381-7451. Park is off US 34 Bus west of town and also has 20 campsites for $5 per night.

Holly	Rest area on US 50 (south side of road) about two miles east of town. Free
Hooper	My Sister's Place at 11704 CO 17
Lake George	Travel Port RV Park on US 24 in Lake George, which is between Colorado Springs and Buena Vista. $5 fee if you are not camping.
Lamar	Lamar Truck Plaza at US 50 and US 287
Lamar	Love's Travel Stop at US 50 and US 287
Leadville	City of Leadville Sanitation on the south side of US 24 near the Colorado Mountain College. $5 fee.
Littleton	Chatfield State Park off US 85 or CO 470, $5. Water is turned off between Labor Day and Memorial Day.
Longmont	Boulder County Fairgrounds one block east of Hover Rd and Rogers Rd/Boston Ave intersection, $5 fee. The fairground also has several RV sites. Open Wed-Sun from 8am to 4pm
Louisville	Louisville Recycle Center on CO 42 just north of Pine St. Dumping is free. Coin-operated water service is available. Closed Sundays.
Lyons	Library Park on US 36 one block east of US 36 and CO 7 junction. Not readily visible. It's across the street from the visitor center.
Meeker	Public dump station is at 6th and Water streets
Monte Vista	Monte Vista Co-op on US 160 about two miles east of Monte Vista
Montrose	Country Village RV Resort, 22045 S US 550, 7 miles south of town, $5 fee if not camping
Montrose	Shell Super Mart on US 50
Nathrop	Chalk Creek Campground on US 285 about 5 miles south of US 24 and US 285 junction. $10 fee if not camping.
Ordway	The Junction at CO 71 and CO 96
Pagosa Springs	The Corner Store Inc at corner of US 160 and Piedra Rd (CR 600), no fee
Paonia	Rest area off CO 133, free. Going north towards Paonia on CO 133, turn right to Paonia at first opportunity. Just after waste treatment facility on right and over a bridge, rest area is on left. Overnights are free as well.
Pueblo	Texaco at southwest corner of US 50 and McCulloch Blvd, 7 miles west of I-25 Exit 101, no fee. Dump station is on the north side of site, next to the car wash.

Rangely	Rangely Camping Park, $5. Park is at the east end of town; turn north off CO 64 at the blue fire station, then turn right in two blocks.
Rocky Ford	A public dump station is at the Loaf'n Jug on US 50 in center of town. $5 fee, free with fuel purchase.
Salida	Salida Chamber of Commerce on east side of the Hot Springs Pool park, right outside the chamber, no charge
Walden	KOA campground on CO 14 about 16 miles southeast of town, $5 fee
Walden	Public dump station at 3rd and Washington, across from city pool, one block east of CO 125, donation accepted

Connecticut

Below is a list of RV dump stations easily accessed along Interstate highways in Connecticut.

Interstate 84

Interstate 84 runs east to west for 98 miles from the Massachusetts state line to the New York state line. Exit numbers are based on the consecutive numbering system rather than the mile marker system. Eastbound travelers should read up the chart. Westbound travelers read down the chart.

Exit(mm)	Description
71	**Ruby Rd**
	TA Travel Center
(85)	Welcome Center (wb)
(42)	Rest Area (eb)
	Comments: Dump station is closed Nov 1 to Apr 1
2	**US 6 / US 202 / Old Ridgebury Rd**
	Welcome Center (eb)

Interstate 91

Interstate 91 runs north to south for 58 miles from the Massachusetts state line to I-95 in New Haven. Exit numbers are based on the consecutive numbering system rather than the mile marker system. Northbound travelers should read up the chart. Southbound travelers read down the chart.

Exit(mm)	Description
(22)	Rest Area (nb)
(15)	Rest Area (sb)

Delaware

Below is a list of RV dump stations in Delaware.

Other Locations

City or Town	Description
Bear	Lum's Pond State Park, 1068 Howell School Rd, 302-368-6989, $5. Park is south of US 40 via US 301/DE 896
Dover	Dover Air Force Base at Bay Rd/Hwy 1 in FamCamp, southeast of the Christmas tree and Transient Ramp. Must have Military/DOD ID to get on base. $3
Dover	Dover Downs Casino at 1131 N DuPont Hwy (US 13), no fee
Seaford	Wastewater treatment facility at Pine St and King St
Smyrna	Rest area north of town on US 13, $5 fee, also accessible from DE 1 Exit 119

Florida

Below is a list of RV dump stations in Florida. Listed first are those easily accessed from Interstate highways followed by those in other locations throughout the state.

Interstate 4

Interstate 4 runs east to west for 134 miles from I-95 in Daytona Beach to I-275 in Tampa. Eastbound travelers should read up the chart. Westbound travelers read down the chart.

Exit(mm)	Description
44	**FL 559 / to Auburndale**
	Love's Travel Stop
10	**CR 579 / Mango / Thonotosassa**
	Flying J Travel Plaza
7	**US 301 / Hillsborough Ave**
	Singh 301

Interstate 10

Interstate 10 runs east to west for 370 miles from I-95 in Jacksonville to the Alabama state line. Eastbound travelers should read up the chart. Westbound travelers read down the chart.

Exit(mm)	Description
303	**US 441 / Lake City**
	Lake City KOA, $6 fee, one mile north of exit.
258	**FL 53 / Madison**
	Yogi Bear's Jellystone Park & RV Resort, $8 fee
	Comments: From exit, go south 200 feet to Old Saint Augustine Rd and then west about 1 mile to park
192	**US 90 / to Tallahassee**
	Flying J Travel Plaza
	Pilot Truck Stop, free. Dump station is adjacent to the large propane tank to the north of the building with plenty of turning room.

31	FL 87 / to Milton
	KOA north of exit, $10 fee

Interstate 75

Interstate 75 runs north to south for 472 miles from the Georgia state line to the junction with FL 826 in Miami. Northbound travelers should read up the chart. Southbound travelers read down the chart.

Exit(mm)	Description
368	CR 318 / Orange Lake
	Petro Stopping Center
285	FL 52 / to Dade City
	Flying J Travel Plaza
9a	FL 820 / Pines Blvd / Pembroke Pines
	C.B. Smith Park (county park), 900 N Flamingo Rd, 954-437-2650. Camping is also available.

Interstate 95

Interstate 95 runs north to south for 382 miles from the Georgia state line to US 1 in Miami. Northbound travelers should read up the chart. Southbound travelers read down the chart.

Exit(mm)	Description
305	FL 206 / to Hastings
	Flying J Travel Plaza
273	US 1
	Texaco Fuel Stop
131b	FL 68 / Orange Ave
	Flying J Travel Plaza
31	FL 816 / Oakland Park Blvd
	Easterlin Park (county park), 1000 NW 38th St, 954-938-0610. Camping is also available.
21	FL 822 / Sheridan St
	Topeekeegee Yugnee Park (county park), 3300 N Park Rd, 954-985-1980. Camping is also available.

Other Locations

City or Town	Description
Bahia Honda Key	Bahia Honda State Park, 36850 Overseas Hwy (US 1), 305-872-2353.
Brooksville	Register Chevrolet, 14181 Cortez Blvd, 352-597-3333. Location along westbound FL 50 across from Register RV. Free
Clearwater	Bay RV Supercenter, 16485 US 19N, on E Service Road (northbound - no direct entrance for southbound travelers), $5 fee, nice place to stop and rest or have repairs done
Clewiston	John Stretch Park on US 27 about 9 miles east of town at Lake Harbor, free. Dump station is between public restrooms and highway near pump station at east entrance to park.
Deerfield Beach	Quiet Waters Park (county park), 401 S Powerline Rd (FL 845), 954-360-1315. Camping is also available.
Haines City	Commercial Truck Terminal at 35647 US 27
Miami	Larry & Penny Thompson Park (county park) campground, 12451 SW 184th St (Eureka Dr), about one mile west of West Dade Expy (FL 821)
Navarre	Emerald Beach RV Park, 8885 Navarre Pkwy (US 98), 850-939-3431, $5 fee
Ochopee	Public dump station at small campground on south side of US 41 near Fiftymile Bend in the Big Cypress National Preserve. $2 donation.
Ohio Key	Sunshine Key Resort on US 1, $10 fee, 305-872-2217
Panama City Bch	PineGlen RV Park on US 98 about 4 miles east of FL 79, just before Alf Coleman Rd. $10
Sunrise	Markham Park (county park), 16001 W State Road 84, 954-389-2000. Camping is also available. Park is located near the junction of I-75 and I-595.

Georgia

Below is a list of RV dump stations in Georgia. Listed first are those easily accessed from Interstate highways followed by those in other locations throughout the state.

Interstate 16

Interstate 16 runs east to west for 167 miles from Savannah to I-75 in Macon. Eastbound travelers should read up the chart. Westbound travelers read down the chart.

Exit(mm)	Description
(46)	Rest Area (wb)
(44)	Rest Area (eb)

Interstate 20

Interstate 20 runs east to west for 202 miles from the South Carolina state line to the Alabama state line. Eastbound travelers should read up the chart. Westbound travelers read down the chart.

Exit(mm)	Description
(201)	Welcome Center (wb)
(182)	Rest Area
114	**US 441 / US 129 / to Madison**
	Pilot Travel Center
(108)	Rest Area (wb)
(103)	Rest Area (eb)
9	**Atlantic Ave / Waco**
	Love's Travel Stop, 770-824-5040

Interstate 75

Interstate 75 runs north to south for 355 miles from the Tennessee state line to the Florida state line. Northbound travelers should read up the chart. Southbound travelers read down the chart.

Exit(mm)	Description
326	**Carbondale Rd**
	Pilot Travel Center
320	**GA 136 / Resaca / to Lafayette**
	Flying J Travel Plaza
(319)	Rest Area (sb)
(308)	Rest Area (nb)
296	**Cassville-White Rd**
	TA Travel Center
201	**GA 36 / to Jackson**
	Flying J Travel Plaza
138	**Thompson Rd**
	Happy Store
135	**US 41 / GA 127/ Perry**
	Perry Welcome Center, 101 General Courtney Hodges Blvd, free
(118)	Rest Area (sb)
(108)	Rest Area (nb)
101	**US 280 / GA 90 / Cordele**
	Pilot Travel Center
(85)	Rest Area (nb)
(76)	Rest Area (sb)
60	**Central Ave / Tifton**
	Pilot Travel Center
(48)	Rest Area (sb)
(47)	Rest Area (nb)
11	**GA 31 / Valdosta**
	Wilco Travel Plaza
5	**GA 376 / Lake Park**
	Eagles Roost RV Resort on Mill Store Rd, $5
2	**Lake Park / Bellville**
	Flying J Travel Plaza

Interstate 85

Interstate 85 runs north to south for 179 miles from the South Carolina state line to the Alabama state line. Northbound travelers should read up the chart. Southbound travelers read down the chart.

Exit(mm)	Description
(176)	Welcome Center (sb)
160	**GA 51 / to Homer**
	Flying J Travel Plaza
	Petro Stopping Center
147	**GA 98 / to Commerce**
	Pilot Travel Center
41	**US 27 / US 29 / Newnan**
	Pilot Travel Center
(.5)	Welcome Center (nb)

Interstate 95

Interstate 95 runs north to south for 113 miles from the South Carolina state line to the Florida state line. Northbound travelers should read up the chart. Southbound travelers read down the chart.

Exit(mm)	Description
102	**US 80 / GA 26 / Pooler**
	Bill Waites RV World; go east of exit and then right at first light; no charge
(41)	Rest Area (sb)
29	**US 17 / US 82 / GA 520 / Brunswick**
	Flying J Travel Plaza
3	**GA 40 / Kingsland / to Saint Marys**
	Pilot Travel Center
1	**Saint Marys Rd**
	Welcome Center (nb)
	Cisco Travel Plaza

Interstate 185

Interstate 185 is about 48 miles long. It runs north to south between I-85 near La Grange and US 27 south of Columbus. Northbound travelers should read up the chart. Southbound travelers read down the chart.

Exit(mm)	Description
12	Williams Rd
	Welcome Center

Interstate 475

Interstate 475 runs north to south for 16 miles. It begins on I-75 at exit 177 and ends at I-75 exit 156, bypassing Macon. Northbound travelers should read up the chart. Southbound travelers read down the chart.

Exit(mm)	Description
(8)	Rest Area (nb)

Other Locations

City or Town	Description
Bainbridge	Inland Travel Center on US 84 just west of Bainbridge at US 27
McCaysville	Rebel's Chevron on GA 5 between Blue Ridge and McCaysville. The dump station is close to the diesel pump and phone booth on the right side of the driveway as you pull in. No charge.
Pelham	Amoco at 317 US 19
Thomasville	Thomasville Travel Center at 2685 US 84 Bypass
Waynesboro	City park off US 25, south end of town, no fee

Idaho

Below is a list of RV dump stations in Idaho. Listed first are those easily accessed from Interstate highways followed by those in other locations throughout the state.

Interstate 15

Interstate 15 runs north to south for 196 miles from the Montana state line to the Utah state line. Northbound travelers should read up the chart. Southbound travelers read down the chart.

Exit(mm)	Description
167	**ID 22 / Dubois**
	Scoggins RV Camp
119	**Grandview Dr / US 20 / Idaho Falls**
	Grandview Texaco
113	**US 26 / to Idaho Falls**
	Yellowstone Truck Stop
108	**E 1250 N / Horseshoe Rd / Shelley**
	North Bingham Recreation Site (County Park)
93	**US 26 / ID 39 / Blackfoot**
	Chevron on Parkway Dr
	Flying J Travel Plaza
71	**Pocatello Creek Rd / Pocatello**
	Bannock County Fairgrounds
	Comments: From exit go east on Pocatello Creek Rd, north on Olympus Dr, and west on Fairway Dr.
	Willie's Chevron
47	**US 30 / McCammon / to Lava Hot Springs**
	McCammon Chevron
31	**ID 40 / to Downey**
	Flags West Truck Stop (fee charged)

Interstate 84

Interstate 84 runs east to west for approximately 276 miles from the Utah state line to the Oregon state line. Eastbound travelers should read up the chart. Westbound travelers read down the chart.

Exit(mm)	Description
216	**ID 77 / ID 25 / to Declo**
	Village of Trees RV Resort at Travel Stop (fee charged)
208	**ID 27 / to Burley**
	Cassia County Fairgrounds, just north of intersection of US 30 and Hiland Ave, free
194	**ID 25 / to Hazelton**
	Greenwood Pioneer Stop (fee charged)
168	**ID 79 / to Jerome**
	Honker's Mini Mart
157	**ID 46 / Wendell**
	Burt Harbaugh Motors on N Idaho St (ID 46), 1 mile north of exit
	Intermountain Motor Homes & RV Park at 1894 Frontage Rd
	RV dump station maintained by the city at 210 S Shohone St, one block west of N Idaho St (ID 46)
	Wendell Gas & Oil
71	**Orchard / Mayfield**
	Boise Stage Stop
54	**US 20 / US 26 / Broadway Ave / Boise**
	Flying J Travel Plaza, 3353 S Federal Way, 208-385-9745
	Comments: Dump is located in an alley between Flying J's main store and a diesel repair shop behind it. There is a large sign painted on the building indicating its location. The dump is fenced in, but it is free. Give your ID to the clerk, sign a ledger, and they will give you the key. Rinse water is available; potable water and air are available nearby.
36	**Franklin Blvd / Nampa**
	Jackson Food Store
29	**US 20 / US 26 / Franklin Rd / Caldwell**
	Flying J Travel Plaza

Sage Travel Plaza (fee charged)

Public dump station next to fairgrounds, free
Comments: Turn south after exiting highway and head
towards town, past the Sage Travel Plaza. Turn on 21st
Ave and proceed to the railroad tracks. Turn left after
crossing tracks. Dump is next to fairgrounds.

Interstate 86

Interstate 86 runs east to west for about 63 miles from I-15 in Pocatello
to I-84 exit 222, east of Heyburn. Eastbound travelers should read up
the chart. Westbound travelers read down the chart.

Exit(mm)	Description
61	**US 91 / Yellowstone Ave / Chubbuck**
	Big Bear Chevron (fee charged)
58	**US 30 / Tank Farm Rd**
	City Water Treatment Plant on Batiste Rd

Interstate 90

Interstate 90 runs east to west for 74 miles from the Montana state line
to the Washington state line. Eastbound travelers should read up the
chart. Westbound travelers read down the chart.

Exit(mm)	Description
49	**Bunker Ave / Kellogg**
	RV dump station on Bunker Ave across from Silver Mountain
	Gondola Base
45	**N Division St / Pinehurst**
	KOA, 801 N Division St, 208-682-3612, fee is around $10
43	**Coeur d'Alene River Rd**
	Exxon Station
15	**Sherman Ave / Coeur d'Alene**
	Big Y Truck Stop
12	**US 95 / Coeur d'Alene**
	Jifi Stop-N-Shop on Appleway Ave
5	**Spokane St / Post Falls**
	Conoco Gas Station and Convenience Store - north on

Spokane St, right on Seltice Way to Conoco on north side of road

| 2 | **Pleasant View Rd** |
| | Flying J Travel Plaza |

Other Locations

City or Town	Description
American Falls	Selcho Oil Company at Madison St and Oregon Trail Rd
Arco	Carroll's Travel Plaza on US 20/26
Ashton	Tourist Information Center on US 20 north of town, $5
Avery	Upper Landing Wayside, 1 mile east of town on Saint Joe River Rd
Blackfoot	An RV dump station is located next to the fire station at 209 W Idaho St
Boise	Jolley's Service on W State St at N 35th St
Boise/Garden City	On The River RV Park on N Glenwood St (ID 44), fee unknown
Boise/Garden City	Stinker Station at corner of Chinden Blvd (US 20/26) and Glenwood St across from the fairgrounds.
Bonners Ferry	Boundary County Fairgrounds off US 2/95
Bonners Ferry	South Hill Chevron on US 2/95 (fee charged)
Buhl	Buhl Visitor Center, on US 30 at the eastern edge of town
Buhl	Oasis Stop N Go at junction of US 30 and Clear Lakes Rd (fee charged)
Burley	Cassia County Fairgrounds, east of town
Caldwell	City Disposal Station at I-84 Business Loop and ID 19 (Simplot Blvd)
Cambridge	County Fairgrounds on US 95 (fee charged)
Cambridge	Idaho Power campgrounds along ID 71 about 30 miles north of Cambridge
Cascade	Harpo's gas station on the west side of ID 55, south end of town. The dump is located behind the gas station. Open year-round (water off in winter). Free
Coeur d'Alene	County Fairgrounds on Dalton Ave north of town off US 95
Driggs	Elsie's Chevron on ID 33
Elk City	Red River Ranger Station about 1/4 mile south of the old Red River Ranger Station half-way between Elk City and Dixie. Free
Emmett	Cenex Station on N Washington (Daytime only)
Emmett	County Fairgrounds at ID 16 and S Johns Ave

Fairfield	City Park at city center
Filer	Twin Falls County Fairgrounds
Franklin	City RV rest area 1/2 mile south of town on US 91
Genesee	City Park at city center
Gooding	RV dump station maintained by the city is on 2nd Ave, 1/2 block west of Main St
Grace	Grace City Park on ID 34
Grangeville	Mountain Top Quick Lube & Gas at 507 W Main St (fee charged)
Grangeville	Rae Brothers Sporting Goods at 247 E Main St (fee charged)
Hailey	City Park at ID 75 and 4th Ave
Hazelton	Hazelton City Park on ID 25 at S Howard St
Homedale	City Park on US 95 by the Snake River on the east side of town
Idaho City	Community Center in town off Montgomery St
Idaho Falls	Beeches Corner Rest Stop on US 26 north of town
Island Park	Public dump station on US 20 south of town in a rest area. There is parking, picnic tables, restrooms, and a dump station with non-potable water. No charge.
Jerome	Jerome County Fairgrounds on W 4th Ave
Kamiah	BJ's Auto Repair just off US 12 in town, $4 fee
Kamiah	Kamiah Shell on US 12 at the east end of town (fee charged)
Kamiah	The Station on US 12 at the west end of town (fee charged)
Kendrick	Public dump station on ID 3 at the east edge of town near the school at the bottom of Kendrick Grade, open seasonally, free.
Ketchum	North of Ketchum, turn east to the Sawtooth NRA Visitor Center. Stay on this road past the visitor center, offices, shops, and residences, then into a large meadow. Dump station is in the meadow, just past first dump station sign. Donation requested.
Kingston	Shoshone Base Camp on Coeur d'Alene River Rd about 28 miles north of Kingston I-90 Exit 43
Lenore	Rest Area on US 12 (free, water is also available)
Lewiston	County Fairgrounds at 13th St and Airway Ave
Lewiston	Dales Boat, Camper and Auto Sales at 615 Thain Rd
Lewiston	Flying J Travel Plaza at junction of US 12 and US 95
Lewiston	Jim Eddy's Auto Clinic at 102 Thain Rd

Lewiston	North Lewiston Dynamart on 6th Ave near junction of US 12 and ID 128
Macks Inn	On US 20 at Macks Inn there is a county sewer building with an RV dump station. It is between mile marker 193 and 194. Free
McCall	Ponderosa State Park, 208-634-2164, $4 (entrance fee). The state park is about two miles northeast of town. When entering McCall, turn east on Park St and continue as Park St becomes Thompson. Turn north on Davis Ave and follow signs to park. Dump is located across road from visitor center.
Meridian	Water Treatment Plant at W Ustick Rd and N Ten Mile Rd
Montpelier	City Park at junction of US 30 and US 89
Moscow	Latah County Fairgrounds north of Moscow Mall on White Ave
Moscow	Moscow U-Haul at 2320 W Pullman Rd (ID 8)
Moscow	Redinger Heating & RV at 719 N Main St (US 95)
Mountain Home	Public dump station on E 12th St S, no charge. Take I-84 Bus to E 12th St, turn north. The dump is down a block on your left. Potable water is also available.
Nampa	Wastewater Treatment Plant at 340 W Railroad St
New Plymouth	Lowell's Mini Market on US 30 (fee charged)
Oakley	City RV park at rodeo grounds south of town
Orofino	Dump station is 1/2 mile west of the Orofino bridge on US 12 next to the Armory building. The dump is maintained by the local Good Sam Club (donation is appreciated).
Paris	Paris City Park on US 89 at city center
Payette	Public dump station at 7th Ave N and US 95
Payette	Poole's General Store at 1537 1st Ave S, just west of US 95
Pierce	Public dump station northern end of town on the main street through town.
Pocatello	Bannock County Fairgrounds
Pocatello	U-Haul at 709 N 5th Ave (I-15 Business Loop)
Preston	Preston City Park on US 91 at S 1st Ave
Rexburg	Ray Oakey Gas & Oil at 279 N 2nd E (fee charged)
Richfield	Dump station maintained by the city is on Main St, 2-1/2 blocks north of US 26/93
Rigby	Bob's Kwik Stop on Farnsworth Way (fee charged)
Rigby	Taylor's Quick Stop on US 20 (fee charged)
Riggins	Chevron Station on US 95
Rogerson	Rogerson Service on US 93

Rupert	Dump station maintained by the city is at 10th St and A St
Saint Anthony	Ray's Texaco on S Bridge St at E 3rd St
Saint Maries	Benewah County Fairgrounds at 23rd St and ID 5
Salmon	Salmon Oil Semi Stop at 500 S Challis St (US 93) (fee charged)
Sandpoint	Bonner County Fairgrounds on Boyer Ave, no fee
Shelley	Public dump station behind Food Shop gas station on north end of town, no charge
Sandpoint	Paul's Chevron near 5th & Cedar (fee charged)
Shoshone	Public dump station off US 93 on W "E" St in miniature park, southern end of town
Soda Springs	City of Soda Springs public dump station one block north of US 30 off Main St. Free
Soda Springs	Quick Stop at 111 N Hooper Ave (ID 34) (fee charged)
Twin Falls	Oasis Pump & Wash at 1135 N Blue Lakes Blvd (US 93) in northern Twin Falls
Weiser	Seventh Street Market at E 7th St and US 95
Wilder	Jackson Food Store at US 95 and ID 19

Illinois

Below is a list of RV dump stations in Illinois. Listed first are those easily accessed from Interstate highways followed by those in other locations throughout the state.

Interstate 39

Interstate 39 runs north to south for about 140 miles from the Wisconsin state line to I-55 exit 164. From Rockford to the Wisconsin state line, the Interstate is also I-90. Northbound travelers should read up the chart. Southbound travelers read down the chart.

Exit(mm)	Description
1	**US 51 / IL 75 / S Beloit**
	Flying J Travel Plaza
3	**Rockton Rd / CR 9 / to Rockton**
	Love's Travel Stop, 815-389-1923, no charge. Dump is on automobile side next to Rockton Rd.
99	**IL 38 / Rochelle**
	Petro Stopping Center

Interstate 55

I-55 runs north to south for 295 miles from Chicago to the Missouri state line. Portions of the Interstate are shared with I-70, I-72, and I-74. Northbound travelers should read up the chart. Southbound travelers read down the chart.

Exit(mm)	Description
241	**CR 44 / N River Rd / Wilmington**
	Public campground in Des Plaines Fish & Wildlife Area
109	**CR 2 / Williamsville**
	Love's Travel Stop, no fee
82	**IL 104 / to Pawnee**
	Auburn Travel Center

Interstate 57

Interstate 57 runs north to south for 358 miles from Chicago to the Missouri state line. Portions of the Interstate are shared with I-64 and I-70. Northbound travelers should read up the chart. Southbound travelers read down the chart.

Exit(mm)	Description
(332)	Welcome Center
283	**US 24 / Gilman**
	R&R RV Sales west of exit, 815-265-7218, $10
160	**IL 33 / IL 32 / Effingham**
	Flying J Travel Plaza
83	**North Ave / CR 42 / Ina**
	Love's Travel Stop, 202 North Ave, 618-437-5275

Interstate 70

I-70 runs east to west for 156 miles from the Indiana state line to the Missouri state line. Portions of the Interstate are also I-55 and I-57. Eastbound travelers should read up the chart. Westbound travelers read down the chart.

Exit(mm)	Description
160	**IL 33 / IL 32 / Effingham**
	Flying J Travel Plaza

Interstate 74

Interstate 74 runs east to west for 221 miles from the Indiana state line to the Iowa state line. Portions of the Interstate are also I-55. Eastbound travelers should read up the chart. Westbound travelers read down the chart.

Exit(mm)	Description
160a	**US 150 / IL 9 / Market St / Bloomington**
	TA Travel Center
(114)	Rest Area
(30)	Rest Area (wb)
(28)	Rest Area (eb)

Interstate 80

Interstate 80 runs east to west for 163 miles from the Indiana state line to the Iowa state line. A small segment is shared with I-94 and I-294. Eastbound travelers should read up the chart. Westbound travelers read down the chart.

Exit(mm)	Description
148a	**Harlem Ave / Tinley Park** Windy City Campground, 18701 80th Ave, 708-720-0030, $12 if not camping. From exit go south to W 191st St; west to S 80th Ave; north to campground.
130	**Larkin Ave / Joliet** Empress Casino and RV Park *Comments*: Dump station is directly behind the hotel, easy entry and exit with tow vehicle, no charge
77	**IL 351 / La Salle** Flying J Travel Plaza
75	**IL 251 / Peru** Tiki Truck Stop

Interstate 90

Interstate 90 runs east to west for 108 miles from the Indiana state line to the Wisconsin state line. Portions of the Interstate are also I-39, I-94, and the Northwest Tollway. Mile markers on the Northwest Tollway *decrease* from west to east, the opposite of the normal numbering system. Eastbound travelers should read up the chart. Westbound travelers read down the chart.

Exit(mm)	Description
26	**Randall Rd / Elgin** Paul Wolff Forest Preserve, $5 if not camping. From exit go south to Big Timber Rd and then west 1.5 miles to park.
3	**Rockton Rd / CR 9 / to Rockton** Love's Travel Stop, 815-389-1923, no charge. Dump is on automobile side next to Rockton Rd.
1	**US 51 / IL 75 / S Beloit** Flying J Travel Plaza

Interstate 94

Interstate 94 runs east to west for 77 miles from the Indiana state line to the Wisconsin state line. Portions are also I-80, I-90 and the Tri-State Tollway. Mile markers on the Tri-State Tollway *decrease* from west to east, the opposite of the usual numbering system. Eastbound travelers should read up the chart. Westbound travelers read down the chart.

Exit(mm)	Description
1	**Russell Rd**
	TA Travel Center

Interstate 270

Interstate 270 forms an open loop around Saint Louis. This portion in Illinois runs east to west from I-70/I-55 to the Missouri state line. Eastbound travelers should read up the chart. Westbound travelers read down the chart.

Exit(mm)	Description
6b	**IL 111 / Pontoon Beach / Mitchell**
	Flying J Travel Plaza, phone: 618-931-1580

Interstate 355

Interstate 355 is a 19-mile route in the Chicago area. It runs north to south between I-290 Exit 7 and I-55 Exit 269. Northbound travelers should read up the chart. Southbound travelers read down the chart.

Exit(mm)	Description
18	**Maple Ave / Downers Grove**
	Downers Grove Sanitary District, 2710 Curtiss St, no charge. From exit go east on Maple Ave, north on Walnut Ave, east on Curtiss St. Non-potable water available. Open regular business hours.

Other Locations

City or Town	Description
Cahokia	Cahokia RV Parque, $10 fee. Campground is at the intersection of IL 3 and IL 157 about two miles north of I-255 Exit 13.
East Saint Louis	Casino Queen RV Park, $5. RV park is at east end of parking lot for Casino Queen on the Mississippi River. Accessible from I-55, I-64, and I-70.
Island Lake	Crystal Valley RV at IL 176 and Darrell Rd, 866-885-7621, $10
Kewanee	Johnson's Salk Trail State Park; dump is inside state park just before campground; no fee
McLeansboro	Hamilton County State Fish & Wildlife Area, 7 miles east of town
Naperville	Wastewater treatment plant at 3712 Plainfield-Naperville Rd, no fee. The site is in southern Naperville between 95th St and 104th St. Accessible from I-55 Exit 263, about 5 miles north of exit.
Salem	Marion County Fairgrounds on IL 37 south of town
Thomson	Tomson Causeway Park (Corps of Engineers), west of town on Mississippi River, $5 fee
Zion	Illinois Beach State Park, no fee. There are two dump stations in the campground and one past the picnic areas just before the main parking lot at the beach. The campground stations are for campers but the one at the picnic area can be used by anyone.

Indiana

Below is a list of RV dump stations in Indiana. Listed first are those easily accessed from Interstate highways followed by those in other locations throughout the state.

Interstate 64

Interstate 64 runs east to west for 124 miles from the Kentucky state line to the Illinois state line. Eastbound travelers should read up the chart. Westbound travelers read down the chart.

Exit(mm)	Description
25b	**US 41 / to Evansville** Flying J Travel Plaza Pilot Travel Center
(7)	Welcome Center (eb)

Interstate 65

Interstate 65 runs north to south for 262 miles from US 12/20 in Gary to the Kentucky state line. Northbound travelers should read up the chart. Southbound travelers read down the chart.

Exit(mm)	Description
175	**IN 25 / Lafayette** Lafayette Travel Trailer Sales, 765-423-5353, $5. Located 1/2 mile west of exit.
139	**IN 39 / Lebanon** Flying J Travel Plaza
99	**Greenwood** Pilot Travel Center
95	**Whiteland Rd / CR 500 / Whiteland** Flying J Travel Plaza

Interstate 69

Interstate 69 runs north to south for 158 miles from the Michigan state line to I-465 exit 37 in Indianapolis. Northbound travelers should read up the chart. Southbound travelers read down the chart.

Exit(mm)	Description
126	**CR 11A**
	Auburn KOA, $5
78	**IN 5 / to Warren**
	Crazy D's
64	**IN 18 / Marion**
	Love's Travel Stop, free

Interstate 70

Interstate 70 runs east to west for 157 miles from the Ohio state line to the Illinois state line. Eastbound travelers should read up the chart. Westbound travelers read down the chart.

Exit(mm)	Description
149b	**US 35 / IN 38 / Richmond**
	Love's Travel Stop
149a	**US 35 / IN 38 / Richmond**
	Tom Raper RVs, 800-727-3778, Free. Dump station is just off Rich Rd, near the Body Shop and Trailers Division building.
123	**IN 3 / Spiceland**
	Flying J Travel Plaza
115	**IN 109 / to Knightstown**
	Gas America

Interstate 74

Interstate 74 runs east to west for 172 miles from the Ohio state line to the Illinois state line. A portion is also shared with I-465. Eastbound travelers should read up the chart. Westbound travelers read down the chart.

Exit(mm)	Description
4	**IN 37 / Harding St**
	Flying J Travel Plaza
(1)	Welcome Center (eb)

Interstate 80

I-80 runs east to west for 152 miles from the Ohio state line to the Illinois state line. Portions are also I-90, I-94, and the Indiana Toll Road. Eastbound travelers should read up the chart. Westbound travelers read down the chart.

Exit(mm)	Description
(126)	Rest Area
(90)	Rest Area
(56)	Rest Area
9a	**Grant St**
	Flying J Travel Plaza

Interstate 90

I-90 runs east to west for about 157 miles from the Ohio state line to the Illinois state line. Portions are also I-80 and the Indiana Toll Road. Eastbound travelers should read up the chart. Westbound travelers read down the chart.

Exit(mm)	Description
(126)	Rest Area
(90)	Rest Area
(56)	Rest Area

Interstate 94

Interstate 94 runs east to west for 46 miles from the Michigan state line to the Illinois state line. A portion is also shared with I-80. Eastbound travelers should read up the chart. Westbound travelers read down the chart.

Exit(mm)	Description
22a	**US 20 / Burns Harbor**
	Pilot Travel Center
9a	**Grant St**
	Flying J Travel Plaza

Interstate 465

Interstate 465 forms a 54-mile loop around Indianapolis. Exit numbering begins at US 31 and increases in a clockwise direction.

Exit(mm)	Description
4	IN 37 / Harding St
	Flying J Travel Plaza

Other Locations

City or Town	Description
Elkhart	United Wastewater Recovery Center at 1143 Oak St, $5 fee
Fort Wayne	Berning Trailer Sales, 5220 New Haven Ave, 260-749-9415, $1 fee. Rinse water available but no potable water. Located about 1/2 mile off US 24/30 between Fort Wayne and New Haven. From I-469 Exit 19, go west about 4 miles.
Fort Wayne	Johnny Appleseed Park & Municipal Campground off IN 930 (Coliseum Blvd) at Parnell Ave, $2, 260-427-6720
Gas City	Gas City Park on Broadway St, contact police dept to pay $1 fee and obtain combination to the lock at the facility
Lawrenceburg	Shell station on US 50 just west of Main St at the Kroger shopping center, $5 fee, fresh donuts made throughout the day!
Logansport	City park near High St and 17th St. From Market St (US 24) in town, go north on 17th St to High St and turn right. Free
Marion	Marion Municipal Utility on Bond Ave, open Mon-Fri 8am to 5pm, no charge, inquire with employee for procedures to follow
Michigan City	S&H RV Superstore, 1615 W US Hwy 20, 219-872-1023, $7.50 donation (goes to local charity)
Peru	Gallahan Travel Plaza at US 31 and US 24

Iowa

Below is a list of RV dump stations in Iowa. Listed first are those easily accessed from Interstate highways followed by those in other locations throughout the state.

Interstate 29

I-29 runs north to south for 152 miles from the South Dakota state line to the Missouri state line. A 4-mile section in Council Bluffs is also I-80. Northbound travelers should read up the chart. Southbound travelers read down the chart.

Exit(mm)	Description
(139)	Welcome Center (sb) / Rest Area (nb)
(110)	Rest Area
(80)	Rest Area (sb)
(78)	Rest Area (nb)
(38)	Rest Area
10	**IA 2 / to Nebraska City**
	Cross Roads Texaco
	Sapp Brothers Truck Stop

Interstate 35

Interstate 35 runs north to south for 219 miles from the Minnesota state line to the Missouri state line. Part of the Interstate is also I-80. Northbound travelers should read up the chart. Southbound travelers read down the chart.

Exit(mm)	Description
(214)	Welcome Center
(159)	Rest Area
(120)	Rest Area (nb)
(119)	Rest Area (sb)
126	**Douglas Ave / Urbandale**
	Pilot Travel Center
(32)	Rest Area
(7)	Welcome Center

Interstate 80

Interstate 80 runs east to west for 307 miles from the Illinois state line to the Nebraska state line. A portion of the Interstate is also I-35. Eastbound travelers should read up the chart. Westbound travelers read down the chart.

Exit(mm)	Description
292	**IA 130 / Northwest Blvd**
	Flying J Travel Plaza
(270)	Welcome Center (wb) / Rest Area (eb)
259	**Springdale / to West Liberty**
	Amoco Travel Plaza
254	**Baker Ave / West Branch**
	Kum 'n Go
	Comments: one-half mile south of Hoover Presidential Library, no charge but you must go inside gas station to ask for the key
(237)	Rest Area
(208)	Rest Area
197	**CR V18 / to Brooklyn**
	Brooklyn 80 Amoco
(180)	Rest Area (dump station in eastbound rest area only)
(147)	Rest Area
126	**Douglas Ave / Urbandale**
	Pilot Travel Center
(119)	Rest Area
(81)	Rest Area (eb)
(80)	Rest Area (wb)
40	**US 59 / Avoca**
	Wings America Travel Center
(19)	Welcome Center (eb) / Rest Area (wb)

Interstate 380

Interstate 380 is a 72-mile spur route off I-80 that connects Iowa City with Waterloo. It is a north/south route. Northbound travelers should read up the chart. Southbound travelers read down the chart.

Exit(mm)	Description
70	**River Forest Rd / Evansdale**
	Deerwood City Park north of exit and west of River Forest Rd, $1 fee
68	**Evansdale Dr**
	Flying J Travel Plaza
(13)	Rest Area

Other Locations

City or Town	Description
Adel	Dallas County Fairgrounds on US 169, north end of town. Dump is located in campground at rear of fairgrounds. Fee unknown
Aurora	Aurora Gas & Goods at CR W45 and CR C57
Cedar Falls	Fogdall RV, 7805 Ace Pl, 800-747-0747, free. Use Exit 225 on US 20. Site is on separate service island before entering main parking area.
Clarinda	Dump site at the Clarinda Airport near S 8th St and La Perla Dr
Clinton	Riverview Park (city park) east of US 67 via 6th Ave S to 19th Ave N at river, no fee
Coon Rapids	City park on North St, west side of town, no fee. Dump is along south side of parking area near restroom, south of swimming pool. No water.
Corning	County park on Lake Icaria 3 miles north of town on IA 148
Corydon	Dump station is on the south side of IA 2 at the east edge of town, no fee
Creston	McKinley Park campground (city park) on Lakeshore Dr
Dubuque	Massey Marina Park (county park), 9400 Massey Ln, 5 miles south of town, no charge if camping, $5 fee if not
Dubuque	Mud Lake Park (county park), 11000 Golf Lake Rd, 7 miles north of town, no charge if camping, $5 fee if not

Dubuque	Swiss Valley Park (county park), 13768 Swiss Valley Rd, 10 miles southwest of town, no charge if camping, $5 fee if not
Dyersville	Amoco One Stop at 630 16th Ave SE, near the intersection of US 20 and IA 136
Dyersville	New Wine Park (county park), 16001 New Wine Park Ln, 5 miles north of town, no charge if camping, $5 fee if not
Forest City	Pammel Park (city park) one block east of US 69 and "J" St, 641-585-4860, no fee, 8 dump stations
Fort Dodge	Kennedy Memorial County Park at 1415 Nelson Ave, north of town
Fort Dodge	Webster County Fairgrounds, 22770 Old Hwy 169
Fredericksburg	Public dump station in front of city garage on the west end of town, north side of US 18, no fee
Hawarden	City park on 13th St one block east of IA 10 (Avenue E). Free. Fresh potable water available.
Hawarden	Oak Grove County Park about 6 miles north of town via CR K-18 (Cherry Ave). Free. Camping and fresh water also available.
Lime Springs	Lime Springs Travel Plaza at US 63 and IA 157
Maquoketa	Horseshoe Pond (city park) on S Main St about one mile off US 61, no fee.
Marshalltown	Riverview City Park at IA 14 and Woodland St, north end of town, no fee, camping available
New Albin	Rest area on IA 26, north edge of town on Minnesota border, no fee
Orange City	Veteran's Memorial Park (city park) campground on Iowa Ave SW
Perry	Pattee City Park on W 3rd St
Red Oak	Legion Park (city park) south of US 34 off IA 48 and Alix St
Sanborn	Miller Park, south of US 18 at Redwood Ave on western end of town, also has a golf course and campground
Sherrill	Finley's Landing (county park), 24500 Finley's Landing Rd, no charge if camping, $5 fee if not
Sibley	Osceola County Fairgrounds on 9th St between 1st Ave W and 2nd Ave W
Sibley	Sam Robinson Memorial Park at 700 11th Ave
Sioux Center	Co-op Gas & Oil at 153 N Main Ave (US 75)
Spencer	Leach Park campground (city park) at 305 4th St SE, free if camping, $2 if not
Spirit Lake	Vick's Corner at IA 9 and IA 86 west of Spirit Lake

Tipton	Municipal dump station located on the west side of the public works building at corner of South St and Lynn St, one block west of IA 38. Rinse water available April thru October. Free
West Bend	Grotto of the Redemption campground on 1st Ave NW off IA 15
Winterset	Fairgrounds on Summit St, southwest of town
Winterset	Winterset City Park campground near 10th St and Court St

Kansas

Below is a list of RV dump stations in Kansas. Listed first are those easily accessed from Interstate highways followed by those in other locations throughout the state.

Interstate 35

I-35 runs north to south for 235 miles from the Missouri state line to the Oklahoma state line. A portion of the Interstate is also the Kansas Turnpike. Northbound travelers should read up the chart. Southbound travelers read down the chart.

Exit(mm)	Description
(175)	Rest Area
127	US 50 / KS 57 / Newton
	Flying J Travel Plaza, 4245 W US 50, 620-343-2717, free

Interstate 70

I-70 runs east to west for 423 miles from the Missouri state line to the Colorado state line. A segment is also the Kansas Turnpike. Eastbound travelers should read up the chart. Westbound travelers read down the chart.

Exit(mm)	Description
411b	I-435 / Kansas City
	Cabela's - Use I-435 Exit 13b
341	KS 30 / Elm Rd / Maple Hill
	Maple Hill Truck Stop
(336)	Rest Area
(310)	Rest Area
295	US 77 / KS 18 / Marysville
	Sapp Brothers Truck Stop
(294)	Rest Area
(265)	Rest Area
253	Ohio St
	Flying J Travel Plaza
252	N 9th St / Salina
	Thomas Park (city park) about 1/2 mile south of exit on west

side of road. Overnight parking is permitted. Fee unknown.
785-309-5765

(224)	Rest Area
206	**KS 232 / Wilson**
	The Waterin' Hole
(187)	Rest Area
(132)	Rest Area
(97)	Rest Area
(48)	Rest Area
17	**KS 27 / Goodland**
	Mid America Camp Inn, 785-899-5431, $5 fee. If office is closed, put money through slot above night registry box. Let fall all the way in (don't leave on shelf).
(7)	Welcome Center (eb) / Rest Area (wb)

Interstate 135

Interstate 135 runs north to south for 95 miles between Salina and Wichita. Northbound travelers should read up the chart. Southbound travelers read down the chart.

Exit(mm)	Description
(68)	Rest Area
40	**Hesston**
	Sav-A-Trip
31	**Newton**
	Newell Truck Plaza
(23)	Rest Area
2	**Hydraulic St / Wichita**
	Wichita Wastewater Treatment Plant on Industrial Dr, one mile north of exit

Interstate 435

Interstate 435 is an 83-mile loop around Kansas City. Exit numbering begins at Lackman Road in Kansas and increases in a clockwise direction.

Exit(mm)	Description
13	**US 24 / State Ave / Kansas City**
	Cabela's, 913-328-0322, free, GPS: N 39° 7.230' W 94° 48.933'

Other Locations

City or Town	Description
Anthony	Coastal Q-Mart at 519 N LL&G Ave (KS Hwy 2)
Arkansas City	Newman Park at 1801 S Summit. Also has 8 RV spaces with electric hookups, picnic shelter, water, grills, and fishing area.
Baxter Springs	City park one mile west of Alt US 69 and US 166
Beloit	City park on KS 14, south end of town, donation requested. Camping is also available with some electric hookups.
Blue Rapids	Riverside Park (city park) on US 77, camping is also available.
Burlington	Drake Park (city park), about 5 blocks east of US 75 on Cross St, north end of town, no fee. Also has campsites with hookups.
Burlington	Kelley Park (city park), one block east of US 75, southern end of town, no fee. Also has campsites with hookups.
Chanute	Santa Fe City Park south end of town near Nu-Wa RV plant, 35th St Pkwy and S Santa Fe St. Free camping for 48-hour period, $3 per night after that.
Chetopa	Dump is near city park, behind fire station on US 166, no fee. Campground with electric hookups available in city park, $5 for RVs
Coffeyville	Walter Johnson Park in town
Deerfield	Country Corner West at US 50 and Main St
Derby	Derby water treatment plant, 1501 S Hwy 15, about one mile south of town on west side of highway. Open Mon-Fri 9am to 5pm, 316-788-1151, free.
Greensburg	The Big Well tourist attraction at Sycamore St and Wisconsin Ave, $3 fee (waived with purchase of two tickets)
Hill City	RV dump is at 901 W Main St (US 24)
Holton	Phillips 66 gas station on US 75 at 5th St in center of town, no fee
Horton	Dump station is on north side of US 73 at east edge of town, site is marked but not too well so be attentive, no fee
Liberal	Arkalon Park, ten miles east of town on US 54, camping available
Liberal	City wastewater treatment plant on US 83 bypass

Lincoln	Public dump station is about one mile south of town on the west side of KS 14, no fee. Visitor comments: "Not much of a site but kind of a welcome place when in dire need"
Marysville	City Park on S 10th St (US 77) at the southern end of town
Meade	City park on US 54 east of town, no fee, fresh water, free overnight parking
Mullinville	Sunflower Plaza at US 54 and Main St
Ottawa	Michigan Valley Park (Corp of Engineers) at Pomona Lake on north end of dam about 18 miles west of town
Perry	Rock Creek Campground (Corps of Engineers) on west side of Perry Lake. Free. Fresh water and flush water also available.
Perry	Slough Creek Campground (Corps of Engineers) on east side of Perry Lake. Free. Fresh water and flush water also available.
Pittsburg	Lincoln Park (city park) on US 69 Bypass at 20th St. Park also has about 8 campsites with electric and water hookups at $10 per night.
Plainville	City RV park along US 183 north of town. Campsites with concrete pads, electric, water, and sewage hookups, $3 per night.
South Hutchinson	Plaza Go at US 50 and S Main St (KS 96)
Stockton	Rooks County fairgrounds
Sublette	Stockade Travel Plaza on US 83
Topeka	Kansas Expocentre Fairgrounds on Topeka Blvd between 17th and 21st streets. Can be reached from I-70 Exit 361A and traveling south or from I-470 Exit 6 and traveling north. $2 fee.
Topeka	Shawnee Lake Park (county park) at campground on east side of lake between SE 29th St and SE 37th St via SE Croco Rd. Phone: 785-267-1156
Tribune	Ampride at KS 96 and KS 27
Ulysses	Behind City Shop on W McDowell Ave at S Main St, coin-operated
Winfield	Fairgrounds at 1105 W 9th Ave (US 160), open year-round
Winfield	Winfield City Lake (Timber Creek Lake) at 103 S City Lake Rd, 9 miles north on US 77 and 6 miles east on CR 8

Kentucky

Below is a list of RV dump stations in Kentucky. Listed first are those easily accessed from Interstate highways followed by those in other locations throughout the state.

Interstate 24

Interstate 24 runs east to west for 94 miles from the Tennessee state line to the Illinois state line. Eastbound travelers should read up the chart. Westbound travelers read down the chart.

Exit(mm)	Description
86	US 41A / to Fort Campbell
	Flying J Travel Plaza
	Pilot Travel Center

Interstate 64

Interstate 64 runs east to west for 192 miles from the West Virginia state line to the Indiana state line. Eastbound travelers should read up the chart. Westbound travelers read down the chart.

Exit(mm)	Description
185	KY 180 / Cannonsburg
	Flying J Travel Plaza
43	KY 395 / Waddy
	Flying J Travel Plaza
	Waddy '76 Travel Plaza

Interstate 65

Interstate 65 runs north to south for 138 miles from the Indiana state line to the Tennessee state line. Northbound travelers should read up the chart. Southbound travelers read down the chart.

Exit(mm)	Description
116	KY 480 / KY 61
	Love's Travel Stop
81	KY 84 / Sonora
	Davis Brothers Travel Plaza

58	**KY 218 / Horse Cave**
	KOA campground, $3
28	**CR 446 / to US 31**
	Camping World
6	**KY 100 / Franklin**
	Pilot Travel Center
2	**US 31 / to Franklin**
	Flying J Travel Plaza

Interstate 75

Interstate 75 runs north to south for 192 miles from the Ohio state line to the Tennessee state line. A portion of it is shared with I-71. Northbound travelers should read up the chart. Southbound travelers read down the chart.

Exit(mm)	Description
171	**KY 14 / KY 16 / Walton**
	Flying J Travel Plaza
120	**Iron Works Pike**
	Kentucky Horse Park campground, 4089 Iron Works Pkwy,
	800-678-8813. Four separate stations, clean with easy access.
41	**KY 80 / London**
	Tourist Information Center next to Mc'Donalds fast food
	restaurant, free
11	**KY 92 / Williamsburg**
	Pilot Travel Center

Other Locations

City or Town	Description
Flemingsburg	Fox Valley Recreation Park (county park) 6 miles
	southeast of town on James Rd off KY 32
Flemingsburg	Wastewater treatment plant on E Water St (KY 32)
Lebanon	Wastewater treatment plant at 700 W Main St, open 7am
	to 3:30pm, see employee for help
Maysville	Maysville River Park (city park) at Main St and Kentucky St
	on the Ohio River, camping available
Paducah	Public Works Department at 1120 N 10th St, by
	appointment, 270-444-8567

Louisiana

Below is a list of RV dump stations in Louisiana. Listed first are those easily accessed from Interstate highways followed by those in other locations throughout the state.

Interstate 10

Interstate 10 runs east to west for 274 miles from the Mississippi state line to the Texas state line. Eastbound travelers should read up the chart. Westbound travelers read down the chart.

Exit(mm)	Description
(270)	Rest Area (wb)
239	**Louisa St / Almonaster Blvd**
	Big Easy Travel Plaza
236	**LA 39 / Claiborne Ave**
	Mardi Gras Truck Stop
139	**LA 77 / Grosse Tete**
	Bayou Texaco Truck Stop
(121)	Rest Area
87	**LA 35 / to Rayne**
	Frog City Travel Plaza
(67)	Rest Area
64	**LA 29 / to Jennings**
	Jennings Travel Center

Interstate 12

Interstate 12 in Louisiana runs east to west for 85 miles from Baton Rouge to Interstate 10 near Slidell. Eastbound travelers should read up the chart. Westbound travelers read down the chart.

Exit(mm)	Description
35	**Pumpkin Center Rd / Hammond**
	Dixie RV SuperStore, free. The dump is located on the north end of the parking lot near the large propane tanks. Camping World nearby.

Interstate 20

Interstate 20 runs east to west for 189 miles from the Mississippi state line to the Texas state line. Eastbound travelers should read up the chart. Westbound travelers read down the chart.

Exit(mm)	Description
(184)	Welcome Center (wb) / Rest Area (eb)
171	**US 65 / Tallulah**
	Love's Travel Stop
(150)	Rest Area
112	**Well Rd**
	Pilot Travel Center
(97)	Rest Area (wb)
(95)	Rest Area (eb)
(58)	Rest Area
5	**US 79 / US 80 / to Greenwood**
	Kelly's Truck Terminal
3	**US 79 / LA 169 / Mooringsport**
	Flying J Travel Plaza
(2)	Welcome Center (eb)

Interstate 49

Interstate 49 runs north to south for 206 miles from I-20 exit 17 in Shreveport to I-10 exit 103 in Lafayette. Northbound travelers should read up the chart. Southbound travelers read down the chart.

Exit(mm)	Description
138	**LA 6 / to Natchitoches**
	Shop-A-Lott
(35)	Rest Area

Interstate 55

Interstate 55 runs north to south for 66 miles from the Mississippi state line to I-10 exit 209. Northbound travelers should read up the chart. Southbound travelers read down the chart.

Exit(mm)	Description
(65)	Welcome Center (sb)

Interstate 59

Interstate 59 in Louisiana runs north to south for 11 miles from the Mississippi state line to I-10/12 in Slidell. Northbound travelers should read up the chart. Southbound travelers read down the chart.

Exit(mm)	Description
(1)	Welcome Center (sb)

Other Locations

City or Town	Description
Blanchard	Polk Salad Park (city park) near the corner of Alexander Ave and Birch Ave. No water available. Free.
DeRidder	Public dump station in P.W. West Park. Dump station is in the southwest corner of the park. From US 171, proceed west on High School Dr. Go about 1/4 mile and turn right into a paved parking lot between a youth center building and a baseball complex. Not too visable from the road. No charge.
Jonesboro	Wooly's One Stop at 1799 S Hudson Ave (US 167)
Oil City	Earl G Williamson Park along LA 1 south of town on Caddo Lake. $2 fee. Camping also available.
Patterson	City Park off US 90. Campsites with full hookups also available.
Pineville	Paradise Grocery on US 165
Saint Rose	Saint Rose Travel Center at 10405 US 61
Springhill	Frank Anthony City Park at 301 Church St, RV sites with full hookups
Vidalia	K Cafe at 4291 US 84

Maine

Below is a list of RV dump stations in Maine. Listed first are those easily accessed from Interstate highways followed by those in other locations throughout the state.

Interstate 95

I-95 runs north to south for 305 miles from the United States/Canada border to New Hampshire. A segment is also the Maine Turnpike. Northbound travelers should read up the chart. Southbound travelers read down the chart.

Exit(mm)	Description
180	**Coldbrook Rd / to Hampden**
	Dysart's Truck Stop, free with fuel purchase
132	**ME 139 / Fairfield**
	Truckers International, $2

Other Locations

City or Town	Description
Augusta	Augusta Sanitary District, 207-622-6184, no charge. Located just south of the Capital Building on the east side of State St. Access is via a narrow but short road towards Kennebec River. Once through the gate, turn right and then back up to the opposite direction.
Bar Harbor	Burwaldo's convenience store at 6 Pleasant St one block west of Main St (ME 3)
Brunswick	Brunswick Sewer District, 207-729-0148, $6 fee, no water. From US 1 take the Cooks Corner exit and turn right (west) at traffic light. Go past Naval Air Station to Jordan Ave and turn right. Follow blue Brunswick Sewer District signs.
Millinocket	Chamber of Commerce Information Center at 1029 Central St, no fee

Maryland

Below is a list of RV dump stations in Maryland. Listed first are those easily accessed from Interstate highways followed by those in other locations throughout the state.

Interstate 70

Interstate 70 runs east to west for 94 miles from Baltimore at Cooks Lane to the Pennsylvania state line. Eastbound travelers should read up the chart. Westbound travelers read down the chart.

Exit(mm)	Description
(39)	Welcome Center near Myersville

Interstate 81

Interstate 81 runs north to south for 12 miles between the Pennsylvania state line and the West Virginia state line. Northbound travelers should read up the chart. Southbound travelers read down the chart.

Exit(mm)	Description
5	**Halfway Blvd**
	AC&T Fuel Center

Interstate 95

Interstate 95 runs north to south for 110 miles from the Delaware state line to the Virginia state line. A portion of it is shared with I-495. Northbound travelers should read up the chart. Southbound travelers read down the chart.

Exit(mm)	Description
109b	**MD 279 / to Elkton**
	TA Travel Center
100	**MD 272 / to North East**
	Flying J Travel Plaza
(37)	Rest Area

25	US 1 / Baltimore Ave
	Cherry Hill Park, 800-801-6449, $7. From exit, south to Cherry Hill Rd, turn right and go north one mile to park on left.

Interstate 97

Interstate 97 in Maryland runs north to south for 17 miles between I-695 in Ferndale and US 50 near Annapolis. Northbound travelers should read up the chart. Southbound travelers read down the chart.

Exit(mm)	Description
10a	Benfield Blvd / Veterans Hwy (MD 3)
	Washington NE KOA, 768 Cecil Ave N, $15 fee. Northbound travelers should use Exit 10.

Other Locations

City or Town	Description
Marbury	Smallwood State Park along MD 224

Massachusetts

Below is a list of RV dump stations in Massachusetts. Listed first are those easily accessed from Interstate highways followed by those in other locations throughout the state.

Interstate 91

Interstate 91 in Massachusetts runs north to south for 55 miles from the Vermont state line to the Connecticut state line. Exit numbers are based on the consecutive numbering system. Northbound travelers should read up the chart. Southbound travelers read down the chart.

Exit(mm)	Description
22	**US 5 / MA 10 / West St / Northbound Exit Only** Diamond RV Centre, 188 West St, 413-247-3144, $15, closed in winter. Note: Southbound travelers use Exit 23.

Interstate 495

Interstate 495 in Massachusetts runs north to south for 120 miles from I-95 Exit 59 near Amesbury to I-95 and MA 25 near Wareham. Exit numbers are based on the consecutive numbering system. Northbound travelers should read up the chart. Southbound travelers read down the chart.

Exit(mm)	Description
53	**Broad St / Merrimac** Wastewater treatment plant, 50 Federal Way, 978-346-9988, $10

Other Locations

City or Town	Description
Agawam	Bondi's Island Treatment Plant, $1 fee. From I-91 Exit 3 in Springfield, follow Route 5 north toward West Springfield
Fairhaven	Fairhaven Dept of Public Works near US 6 and MA 240, just past the Stop & Shop.

Gloucester	Water treatment facility on MA 127 between Stage Fort Park and Annisquam Bridge, $5 fee. May be used by residents only.
Lowell	Wastewater treatment facility on MA 110 between Lowell and Lawrence, no fee
New Bedford	Wastewater Treatment Plant at Fort Rodman in New Bedford
Newburyport	Wastewater treatment plant, 157 Water St, on waterfront, small location, $5-10 fee
Salem	South Essex Sewerage Plant, 50 Fort Ave, 978-744-4550, no charge. Plant is near Winter Island Park
Taunton	Massasoit State Park, 1361 Middleboro Ave, 508-822-7405, $15 fee, park is 3 miles west of I-495 exit 5

Michigan

Below is a list of RV dump stations in Michigan. Listed first are those easily accessed from Interstate highways followed by those in other locations throughout the state.

Interstate 69

Interstate 69 runs north to south for 203 miles from Port Huron to the Indiana state line. Portions are shared with I-94 and I-96. Northbound travelers should read up the chart. Southbound travelers read down the chart.

Exit(mm)	Description
184	**MI 19 / to Emmett** Bisco's Truck Stop
155	**MI 24 / S Lapeer Rd** Water Tower Park (city park) at 1552 N Main St, $3 fee, 2 1/2 miles north of exit on north end of town
81	**Francis Rd / I-96 West / Grand Ledge** Flying J, 7800 W Grand River Ave, free

Interstate 75

I-75 runs north to south for 395 miles from the United States/Canada border to the Ohio state line. Northbound travelers should read up the chart. Southbound travelers read down the chart.

Exit(mm)	Description
290	**Mill St / Airport Rd / Vanderbilt** Andy's Mobile, $10 fee
251	**Four Mile Rd** Charlie's Country Corner, $4
151	**E Washington Rd / MI 81 / Saginaw** Flying J Travel Plaza
144	**Bridgeport** TA Travel Center, 989-777-7650, $2 fee
101	**Grange Hall Rd / to Holly** Yogi Bear's Jellystone Park of Holly, $5 fee. The dump station is outside the park's gate on the exit side of the drive. In winter there is a drop bax at the office door for the fee.

79   **University Dr / Pontiac**
           A&S RV Center, 2375 N Opdyke Rd, 248-373-5811, call for
           hours, $7
                 Comments: From exit follow University Dr west .2 miles to
                 N Opdyke Rd and turn right (north). Travel north one mile
                 to dealership, which will be on your left.

63   **12 Mile Rd / Madison Heights**
           Oakland County Sewage Disposal System, 29132 Stephenson
           Hwy, 248-544-4694, open 7:30-3:30 Mon-Fri (except when
           raining), free

Interstate 94

Interstate 94 runs east to west for 275 miles from Port Huron to the
Indiana state line. A portion of it is shared with I-69. Eastbound travelers
should read up the chart. Westbound travelers read down the chart.

Exit(mm)	Description
190	**Belleville Rd / Belleville**
	Walt Michaels RV Center, 44700 I-94 Service Dr, $5
159	**MI 52 / Main St / Chelsea**
	Mobil Gas Station, $2 fee
	Comments: Dump is free with fill up of gas or propane

Interstate 96

Interstate 96 is 191 miles long. It runs east to west from I-75 in Detroit
to US 31 near Muskegon. A portion of it is shared with I-69 and I-275.
Eastbound travelers should read up the chart. Westbound travelers read
down the chart.

Exit(mm)	Description
90	**W Grand River Ave / Grand Ledge / Lansing**
	Flying J, 7800 W Grand River Ave, free
52	**MI 50 / Alto / Lowell**
	R2C Road Service, $5 fee
	Comments: Site is two miles south of exit at 6445 Alden Nash (MI 50). Honor system if no one available.

Interstate 275

Interstate 275 in Michigan runs north to south for about 29 miles from I-96 to I-75 Exit 20 in the Detroit area. Northbound travelers read up the chart. Southbound travelers read down the chart.

Exit(mm)	Description
25	**MI 153 / Ford Rd / Westland** Feisters RV, 37401 Ford Rd, $5

Other Locations

City or Town	Description
Bay City	Public dump station at the fairgrounds east of town about two blocks north of MI 25, $2 fee. Use last gate. Turn around after dumping as it may be difficult to get out of fairgrounds.
Bruce Crossing	City park behind Settlers Food Store at MI 28 and US 45, $5. Campsites with water and electric hookups also available for donation.
Cedar River	J.W. Wells State Park along MI 35, $6 (entrance fee to park)
Clare	City park about one mile south of US 10 on west side of Business US 27, $2 fee
Detroit	Detroit wastewater treatment plant, 9300 W Jefferson, free
Harbor Beach	North Park (city park) campground at 836 N Lakeshore Rd, off MI 25 north of town
Howard City	Public dump station at the city's maintenance garage, donation accepted. From US 131, go east on MI 82 about two miles to traffic light. Continue east another block; go south to garage on west side of street; may have to go around block to position RV for dumping.
Hudsonville	Fairgrounds at 5235 Park Ave, open daylight hours during the week
Ironwood	Tourist Park (city park) on US 2, west end of town, fee unknown. The dump site is located just off the highway as you pull into the park on the left side of the road.
Kalamazoo	Kalamazoo County Fairgrounds, no charge. From I-94 Exit 81 (westbound travelers), follow Business Loop I-94 to Lake St and turn east. Follow Lake St to fairgrounds.

	Eastbound I-94 travelers use Exit 80 and go north on Sprinkle Rd to I-94 Bus; west on I-94 Bus to Lake St.
Lowell	Wastewater treatment plant at 300 Bowes Rd, south of MI 21 off Broadway St
Manton	Lake Billings Campground (city park), 231-824-3572, $3. From US 131 and Main St, go east two blocks on E Main St and then north on Park St. Open mid-April to mid-October.
Marquette	Tourist Park (city park) 1/2 mile north of Wright St on Sugar Loaf Ave, $2 fee. 100 RV sites with hookups also available. 906-228-0465
Marshall	Calhoun County Fairgrounds (269-781-8161) at Fair St and S Marshall Ave, $5. Camping is also available. Can be accessed from I-69 Exit 36 or I-94 Exit 110.
Menominee	City park on Menominee River off US 41. Entrance road is between Angeli's Grocery Store and K-Mart. $5
Mount Pleasant	Wastewater treatment plant at 1301 N Franklin St, west of MI 20 and Mission St, no fee
Muskegon	Fishermans Landing campground on Ottawa St west of US 31 Bus, $10 fee
Ontonagon	Ontonagon Township Park on Lakeshore Dr, 906-884-2930, $4
Sandusky	Public dump station in front of the city garage on MI 46 at the east end of town, next to auto parts store. Free
Shepherd	Public dump station maintained by the city about 3 blocks west of US 127. Free.
Sturgis	Sturgis Municipal Airport, northwest of town, free, located on entrance road to hangers, look for sign
Tawas	Tawas RV Park, 1453 Townline Rd, 989-362-0005, $5 fee, 2 miles west of US 23 on Townline Rd, southern end of town
Trenton	Marathon Gas Station at intersection of Van Horn Rd and W Jefferson Ave, just east of Chrysler engine plant, no fee
Wellston	Coolwater Campground, 9424 W 48 1/2 Rd (Hoxeyville Rd), 231-862-3481, $5. Campground is two miles south of MI 55 and 1.5 miles east of MI 37.

Minnesota

Below is a list of RV dump stations in Minnesota. Listed first are those easily accessed from Interstate highways followed by those in other locations throughout the state.

Interstate 35

Interstate 35 runs north to south for 260 miles from Duluth to the Iowa state line. I-35 splits south of Minneapolis into I-35E and I-35W. It comes together again north of Minneapolis. Northbound travelers should read up the chart. Southbound travelers read down the chart.

Exit(mm)	Description
249	**S Boundary Ave / Proctor**
	Holiday Gas Station, 9314 W Skyline Pkwy, 218-628-8000, free
	Comments: Lots of room for big rigs, also sells LP
214	**MN 73 / CR 137 / Moose Lake**
	Moose Lake City Park (218-485-4761) on Birch Ave and 3rd St about 2.5 miles northwest of exit, fee unknown.
	Red Fox Campground (218-485-0341) located between the AmericInn and the Conoco gas station, open May thru August, fee unknown.
169	**Hillside Ave / MN 324 / Pine City**
	Pump N Munch, 1120 Hillside Ave
135	**CR 22 / US 61 / Wyoming**
	Citgo gas station west of exit, next to McDonald's. $3 fee or free with fill-up.
131	**W Broadway Ave / CR 2 / Forest Lake**
	BP Amoco gas station east of exit, free with fill-up or $4 without. Dump is located behind building.
69	**MN 19 / to Northfield**
	Big Steer Travel Center
	Comments: The site dumps into a tank that must be pumped out. A visitor had the unfortunate experience of finding that the tank was completely full.
45	**NW 46th St / Clinton Falls**
	Cabela's, 507-451-4545, free, GPS: N 44° 08.103' W 93° 14.965'
	Comments: In parking lot, separate faucet for potable water, a lot of room and separate entrance for RVs.

42a	US 14 / Owatonna
	Wastewater treatment plant at 1150 Industrial Rd about one mile east of exit off US 14, no charge, open 24 hours
11	CR 46 / Albert Lea
	TA Travel Center

Interstate 90

Interstate 90 runs east to west for 277 miles from the Wisconsin state line to the South Dakota state line. Eastbound travelers should read up the chart. Westbound travelers read down the chart.

Exit(mm)	Description
233	MN 74 / Saint Charles
	Amish Market Square
119	US 169 / Blue Earth
	Faribault County Fairgrounds, no fee. From exit go south to Fairgrounds Rd; turn right; go to entrance and follow signs for camping.
73	US 71 / Jackson
	Burger King restaurant parking lot, free
45	MN 60 Worthington
	Blue Line Travel Center

Interstate 94

Interstate 94 runs east to west for 259 miles from the Wisconsin state line to the North Dakota state line. A portion of it is shared with I-694. Eastbound travelers should read up the chart. Westbound travelers read down the chart.

Exit(mm)	Description
207	MN 101 / Rogers
	TA Travel Center
	Comments: The dump site is located behind the main building. There is also a Camping World about one block away.
178	MN 24 / Clearwater
	Clearwater Travel Plaza, free with fuel purchase, $5 without

171	**CR 7 / CR 75 / Saint Augusta**
	Holiday Station
	Pleasureland RV Center, 25064 20th Ave, 800-862-8603, free
147	**MN 238 / 8th St S / Albany**
	Holiday gas station next to car wash, free
135	**CR 13 / S 2nd Ave E / Melrose**
	Sauk River Park (city park) on N 5th Ave E (CR 13), just north of Main St
103	**MN 29 / Alexandria**
	Tom Thumb Amoco, free with fuel purchase, otherwise $3 fee
54	**MN 210 / Fergus Falls**
	Holiday Station one mile east of exit, free with fuel purchase, might be tight for large RVs
50	**CR 88 / CR 52**
	Interstate Fuel & Food
24	**MN 34 / Barnesville**
	Wagner City Park campground

Interstate 694

Interstate 694 in Minnesota forms a partial loop around Minneapolis/ Saint Paul. It is about 30 miles long and connects I-94 Exit 249 with I-94 near Exit 215. It primarily runs east to west. Portions of it are also shared with I-94 and I-35E. Eastbound travelers should read up the chart. Westbound travelers read down the chart.

Exit(mm)	Description
43a	**Lexington Ave N / Shoreview**
	Shoreview Exxon, free with fill-up

Other Locations

City or Town	Description
Aitkin	City park campground north of MN 210 on 4th Ave NW at Mississippi River, $3. Park has 10 sites with electric hookups.
Akeley	City park along MN 34 on the west side of town, $2. Open Memorial Day to Labor Day. Camping is also available.
Apple Valley	Lebanon Hills Regional Park (county park), 12100 Johnny Cake Ridge Rd, $8 fee. Park is east of MN 77 via CR 38

	(McAndrews) to Johnny Cake Ridge Rd, then north 1.5 miles.
Babbitt	Public dump station across from the fire department on North Dr.
Baudette	Howard's Conoco on Main St (MN 11)
Baudette	Outback Jax on Main St (MN 11)
Bemidji	StaMart Truck Plaza at US 2 and US 71
Bigfork	Public dump station on MN 38 behind only tavern in town. Free will offering. Pay in tavern.
Blaine	Exxon Wash & Fill at MN 65 and 129th Ave, free with fillup, $5 without. Dump is located on the back side of the building. Get access key from attendant.
Bovey	City-maintained dump station on US 169 between Coleraine and Bovey, $3 fee
Brainerd	Lum Park Campground (city park) east of town just off MN 210; 18-site campground; fee unknown
Brainerd	Pine Square Conoco Gas Station on east side of town about one mile south of MN 210 on MN 25. $5 fee. Location also has propane, groceries, and food service.
Buffalo	Co-op gas station at intersection of MN 55 and 8th St NE (CR 35), $10 fee. Dump site goes into a tank that must be pumped out, hence the fee. They also sell propane. No water for rinsing. It has been broken for a year and they do not intend to fix it. It is a poorly run station in general.
Coon Rapids	Phillips 66 near junction of US 10 and Hanson Blvd, $3 without fuel purchase, non-potable water available.
Crookston	Ampride at 1020 Old Hwy 75
Crookston	Crookston Civic Ice Arena, 220 E Robert St (US 2), two blocks from city campground
Cross Lake	Moonlite Square Conoco; north of town at intersection of CR 66 and CR 16; fee unknown
Dawson	Public dump station on US 212 at the Dawson Wayside Rest Area one block south of US 212. Free.
Deer River	Deer River Cenex Convenience Store at US 2 and MN 6
Dundee	Fury's Island County Park on East Graham Lake, 4 miles south of town
Dundee	Maka-Oicu County Park on West Graham Lake south of town
Ely	Public dump station at chamber of commerce, junction of MN 169 and MN 1 east end of town, $3
Farmington	Dakota County Fairgrounds at southwest corner of MN 3 (Chippendale Ave) and MN 50 (Ash St)

Grand Marais	Grand Marais Recreation Area (municipal park), 800-998-0959, fee unknown. Park is located off MN 61 and 8th Ave W.
Hastings	City public works building, no fee. From US 61 in town, go east on 10th St about one mile through industrial area to public works building and turn right. Dump is marked. You must turn around in lot and face north to use dump station.
Hoyt Lakes	Phillips 66 on CR 110
Jackson	Loon Lake area county parks, 11 miles southwest of town, west of US 71 via CR 4
Kandiyohi	Kandiyohi County Park #3 on Diamond Lake, 6920 CR 4 NE, 9 miles northeast of town via US 12 and CR 4
Lake Lillian	Kandiyohi County Park #1 on Kandiyohi Lake, 14391 45th St SE (CR 81), 3 miles east of US 71 via 150th Ave SE (CR 82)
Lake Lillian	Kandiyohi County Park #2 on Kandiyohi Lake, 9122 123rd Ave SE, 5 miles north of town via CR 8
Lakeville	Gas station 1/2 mile east of town on MN 50, no fee
Little Falls	Champs Convenience Center on MN 27 just east of US 10
Little Falls	Zarns Oil Company at US 10 and Haven Rd (CR 76)
Lutsen	Cascade River State Park, 3481 W Hwy 61, 218-387-3053, $3
Mankato	Gag's Camper Way, 507-345-5858, $2.50. Dealer is two miles south of Mankato on US 169 and MN 60.
Mankato	Public dump station on North River Dr, free. From US 169, turn east on Webster Ave and then immediately turn right onto N River Dr. Road ends at dump station.
Marshall	Ampride at US 59 and MN 23
Mora	County fair grounds about two blocks north of MN 65 and S Union St intersection on south end of town, no fee.
Motley	El Ray Travel Plaza, 265 W Hwy 10, 218-352-6784, $6 or free with fuel purchase
Mounds View	Holiday Station at County Road 10 and Silver Lake Road, no fee. Site is 2 miles west of I-35W Exit 28b. County Road 10 is not the same as US 10, which is nearby.
Mountain Iron	Little Joe's Gas Station on US 69, $3 or free with fill-up. Dump station is by the car wash.
Nashwauk	City park on MN 65, north end of town
New London	Kandiyohi County Park #7 on Games Lake, 20944 CR 5 NW, 9 miles west of town via MN 9 and CR 5
Onamia	Public dump station next to visitor center by the water tower, free

Pequot Lakes	A-Pine Express on MN 371 at CR 16, two miles north of town, $3 or free with $20 purchase
Perham	Perham Oasis at US 10 and MN 78
Pipestone	Watertower Park (city park) on 2nd St NE one block west of US 75, no charge, water available
Princeton	Conoco service station at US 169 and LaGrande Ave, $5. Dump is behind the car wash.
Princeton	Public dump station in Mark Park (city park) at 4th St S and 11th Ave S. Non-potable water available. Free.
Prior Lake	Dakota Meadows RV Park & Campground (800-653-2267) next to Mystic Lake Casino, fee unknown.
Rochester	Wastewater treatment plant on 37th St (CR 22) between US 52 and US 63, north end of town, $1 fee, large concrete turnaround, unmanned and open 24/7
Rosemount	Public dump station at city garage one block east of MN 3 on 145th St and then north on Brazil Rd. Free
Sebeka	City park on US 71, $3
Silver Bay	City waste disposal station of MN 61, free. Turn west off MN 61 at lights and follow signs for overlook.
Swan River	One Stop Travel Plaza at US 2 and MN 65
Thief River Falls	Dump is on Oakland Park Rd adjacent to Pioneer Village
Willmar	Sunray Square Phillips 66 just north of town where US 71 and MN 23 merge, $5. They also offer overnight parking with electrical hookups in a well-lit location. Also a nice cafe and deli.
Willmar	Willmar City Sewage Plant on Willmar Ave east of First St (US 71 Bus).
Windom	Island Park (city park) south end of town just west of US 71, no fee. Camping available (10 sites, $10 per night with electricity).
Worthington	Olson Park (city park) campground, 951 Crailsheim Rd, two miles from I-90 Exit 42 via MN 266 and CR 35

Mississippi

Below is a list of RV dump stations in Mississippi. Listed first are those easily accessed from Interstate highways followed by those in other locations throughout the state.

Interstate 10

Interstate 10 runs east to west for 77 miles from the Alabama state line to the Louisiana state line. Eastbound travelers should read up the chart. Westbound travelers read down the chart.

Exit(mm)	Description
(74)	Welcome Center (wb)
(63)	Rest Area
44	**Cedar Lake Rd / to Biloxi**
	Pilot Travel Center
31	**Canal Rd / to Gulfport**
	Flying J Travel Plaza
	Love's Travel Stop
(2)	Welcome Center

Interstate 20

Interstate 20 runs east to west for 154 miles from the Alabama state line to the Louisiana state line. Portions are shared with I-59 and I-55. Eastbound travelers should read up the chart. Westbound travelers read down the chart.

Exit(mm)	Description
(164)	Welcome Center (wb)
129	**US 80 / Lost Gap**
	Spaceway Truck Stop
(90)	Rest Area (eb)
(75)	Rest Area (wb)
68	**MS 43 / Pelahatchie**
	Super Stop
47	**US 49 / Flowood**
	Flying J Travel Plaza
	Pilot Travel Center

11	US 80 / Bovina
	Bovina Truck Stop

Interstate 55

Interstate 55 runs north to south for 291 miles from the Tennessee state line to the Louisiana state line. A small portion is shared with I-20. Northbound travelers should read up the chart. Southbound travelers read down the chart.

Exit(mm)	Description
(279)	Welcome Center (sb)
(276)	Rest Area (nb)
(240)	Rest Area
174	**MS 35 / MS 430 / Vaiden**
	Vaiden KOA Shell
(173)	Rest Area (sb)
(163)	Rest Area (nb)
119	**MS 22**
	Love's Travel Stop
(54)	Rest Area
51	**Sylvarena Rd / to Wesson**
	County Junction Truck Stop
(3)	Welcome Center (nb)

Interstate 59

Interstate 59 runs north to south for 172 miles from the Alabama state line to the Louisiana state line. A portion of it is shared with I-20. Northbound travelers should read up the chart. Southbound travelers read down the chart.

Exit(mm)	Description
(164)	Welcome Center (sb)
113	**MS 528 / to Heidelberg**
	JR's I-59 Truck Stop
67a	**US 49 / MS 42 / Hattiesburg**
	Hattiesburg Convention & Visitors Bureau, free
(3)	Welcome Center (nb)

Other Locations

City or Town	Description
Booneville	Adjacent to West Side City Park on Harold T. White Dr
Carthage	Bud's Place at MS 25 and MS 35
Clarksdale	Fairgrounds at 1150 Wildcat Dr, west of town off MS 322
Columbia	Shell Food Mart at 626 US 98
Hattiesburg	Multipurpose center at 962 Sullivan Dr and US 49, no fee
Lucedale	Four Mile Truck Stop east of Lucedale at 12250 US 98
Lumberton	Little Black Creek Water Park campground, 7 miles north of town, west of US 11
Monticello	Atwood Water Park east of town on US 84, 601-587-2711
Mooreville	Woco at US 78 and MS 371
Olive Branch	Flying J Travel Plaza at US 78 and Bethel Road
Philadelphia	Burnside County Park 5 miles north of town on MS 15
Quitman	Archusa Water Park at 540 CR 110, east of US 45 via MS 511
Starkville	Oktibbeha County Lake Campground about eight miles west of town via US 82 and County Lake Rd, no fee
Tremont	Welcome Center on westbound US 78 just after entering the state from Alabama, about 2 to 3 miles into Mississippi, no fee
Wiggins	Flint Creek Water Park campground on MS 29, northeast of town

Missouri

Below is a list of RV dump stations in Missouri. Listed first are those easily accessed from Interstate highways followed by those in other locations throughout the state.

Interstate 29

Interstate 29 in Missouri runs north to south for 124 miles from the Iowa state line to I-70 in Kansas City. A small segment is also I-35. Northbound travelers should read up the chart. Southbound travelers read down the chart.

Exit(mm)	Description
44	**US 169 / Saint Joseph**
	Love's Travel Stop; dump station is located in the northwest corner of lot near fuel pump stations

Interstate 35

Interstate 35 runs north to south for 115 miles from the Iowa state line to the Kansas state line. Portions are also shared with I-29 and I-70. Northbound travelers should read up the chart. Southbound travelers read down the chart.

Exit(mm)	Description
114	**US 69 / to Lamoni**
	Walter Brothers
54	**US 36 / Cameron**
	Jones Travel Mart

Interstate 44

Interstate 44 runs east to west for 291 miles from I-55 in Saint Louis to the Oklahoma state line. Eastbound travelers should read up the chart. Westbound travelers read down the chart.

Exit(mm)	Description
226	**MO 185 / Sullivan**
	Flying J Travel Plaza

163	**MO 28 / to Dixon**
	Voss Truck Port
123	**Dove Rd**
	KOA Campground, $10
88	**MO 125 / Strafford**
	Speedy's Phillips 66
11a	**US 71 / MO 249 / to Neosho**
	Flying J Travel Plaza
4	**MO 43 / to Seneca**
	Love's Travel Stop

Interstate 55

Interstate 55 runs north to south for 210 miles from the Illinois state line to the Arkansas state line. Northbound travelers should read up the chart. Southbound travelers read down the chart.

Exit(mm)	Description
174b	**US 67 / Festus**
	One Stop, 2285 US 67, $4. Dump station is about two miles southwest of exit just past Buff's RV.
58	**MO 80 / Matthews**
	Flying J Travel Plaza
19	**US 412 / MO 84 / Hayti**
	Pilot Travel Center

Interstate 70

Interstate 70 runs east to west from the Illinois state line to the Kansas state line. It is 252 miles long. Eastbound travelers should read up the chart. Westbound travelers read down the chart.

Exit(mm)	Description
188	**MO A / MO B / to Truxton**
	Flying J Travel Plaza
148	**US 54 / Kingdom City**
	Petro Stopping Center
121	**US 40 / Midway**
	Midway Auto & Truck Plaza
49	**MO 13 / to Higginsville**
	Pilot Travel Center

28	**MO H / MO F / Oak Grove**
	TA Travel Center
24	**US 40 / Grain Valley**
	Apple Travel Trailer Center

Other Locations

City or Town	Description
Aurora	Wastewater Treatment Plant on Highway 39 (open Mon thru Fri, 7am to 4pm, phone: 417-678-3050)
Carthage	T's Corner at 2807 S Grand Ave (MO 571)
Columbia	Cottonwood RV Park, 5170 N Oakland Gravel Rd, 573-474-2747, $5. From I-70 follow US 63 north 4 miles to Prathersville Rd and turn east. Go about 1/4 mile and turn south, park is about 1/2 mile south.
Dixon	Boiling Spring Campground, 18500 Cliff Rd, 573-759-7294, free, open mid-April thru mid-November. Campground is 6 miles north of I-44 Exit 163 via MO 28 and Hwy PP.
Fredericktown	Near City Hall on Buford St
Golden	Viney Creek State Park, no fee. From Golden, go east to Highway "J" and turn north. Go about 4 miles. It is just before the entrance to state park.
Hannibal	Public dump station on north side of Warren Barret Dr just west of Admiral Coontz Armory
Hermitage	Phillips 66 station one block west of US 54 and MO 254 junction
Higginsville	Fairground Park at the park maintenance building (840 W 29th St) behind a Subway store
Kirksville	Shockey's Amoco on US 63 just north of Kirksville
Lamar	Lamar City Park on the west end of the park near camping area
Mexico	Lakeview Park. Approaching town from the south on US 54 Bus, turn left (west) on Lakeview St. Go about 4-5 blocks, turn left on Fairground St. Entrance to Lakeview Park is on the left. Dump is on the first right turn.
Neosho	City of Neosho RV Park, north of town on US 60 Bus (N College St), camping is $12 per night, dump is free and open to public
Nevada	Jump Stop at US 71 and Austin Blvd

Osceola	Osceola RV Park, $2 fee. From MO 13 follow Bus 13 to Parkview Dr and turn north.
Ozark	Big Al's Texaco at US 65 and MO Hwy CC/J
Peculiar	Flying J Travel Plaza off US 71 at MO Hwy J exit
Rolla	Huffman Mobile Homes at 1349 E Hwy 72, phone: 573-364-4242

Montana

Below is a list of RV dump stations in Montana. Listed first are those easily accessed from Interstate highways followed by those in other locations throughout the state.

Interstate 15

I-15 runs north to south for 398 miles from the United States/Canada border to the Idaho state line. A portion of it is also shared with I-90. Northbound travelers should read up the chart. Southbound travelers read down the chart.

Exit(mm)	Description
339	**I-15 Bus / Main St / Conrad**
	Cenex gas station on Main St in center of town, no fee.
290	**US 89 / MT 200 / Vaughn**
	Valley Country Store at 133 US 89, no fee
280	**Central Ave W / Great Falls**
	Holiday Stationstore, 601 Northwest Bypass, free
	Comments: From exit go east to 6th St NW and then north to Northwest Bypass
278	**US 89 / Country Club Blvd / Great Falls**
	Sinclair service station on Fox Farm Rd. Free with fuel purchase. Propane also available.
	Holiday Stationstore, 1601 Fox Farm Rd, free
200	**Lincoln Rd / Helena**
	Lincoln Road RV Park about one mile west of exit, $5
193	**Cedar St / Helena**
	Cenex gas station at Custer Ave and N Montana Ave, no charge. From exit, go west to N Montana St; go north to Custer Ave. Dump station is entered at northwest corner of station lot.
192	**US 12 / US 287 / Helena**
	High Country Travel Plaza
164	**MT 69 / Boulder**
	Boulder City Park on Main St
	Comments: There is no charge for use of RV dump but donations are accepted. City park also has free overnight parking, water, and restrooms with flush toilets.

63	I-15 Bus Route / Dillon
	Rocky Mountain Supply (Cenex station), 700 N Montana St, $5 or free with $10 purchase.

Interstate 90

Interstate 90 is about 552 miles long. It runs east to west from the Wyoming state line to the Idaho state line. A portion is shared with I-15. Eastbound travelers should read up the chart. Westbound travelers read down the chart.

Exit(mm)	Description
495	**MT 47 / Hardin**
	Flying J Travel Plaza
455	**Johnson Ln**
	Flying J Travel Plaza
437	**US 212**
	Pelican Truck Plaza
434	**US 212 / US 310 / Laurel**
	Cenex gas station, dump site is behind store, fee not known
306	**US 10 / N 7th Ave / Bozeman**
	Conoco Grantree Convenience Store, $3 charge, free with fill-up
298	**Jackrabbit Ln / Belgrade**
	Rocky Mountain Supply Co, 350 Jackrabbit Ln
278	**MT 2 / Three Forks**
	Mable's Laundry
	Comments: From I-90 exit go south into town, first business on the left, Milwaukee Espresso in the front parking lot, parking in rear for RVs, $5 fee for dump station use
184	**Boulder Rd / I-90 Bus Route / Deer Lodge**
	Pizza Hut
	Comments: Site is one mile from exit at 202 N Main St (I-90 Bus)
101	**US 93 / Reserve St / Missoula**
	Bretz RV & Marine, 406-541-4800, Free
	Deano's Travel Plaza
	Harvest States Cenex

96	US 93 / MT 200W / Kalispell
	Crossroads Travel Center
	Muralt's Travel Plaza

Interstate 94

Interstate 94 runs east to west from the North Dakota state line to I-90 near Billings. It is about 250 miles long. Eastbound travelers should read up the chart. Westbound travelers read down the chart.

Exit(mm)	Description
138	MT 58 / Miles City
	Cenex General Store

Other Locations

City or Town	Description
Anaconda	Thrifty Gas Station, east end of town, free. Gas station is next to Albertson grocery store. Dump is in back of station. Drinking water available on east side of building.
Bigfork	Washboard Laundromat in strip mall on west side of MT 35 in center of town. Potable water. Not much room for large rigs. Fee unknown.
Chester	Rest area on north side of US 2 near town, donation accepted
Columbia Falls	Mike's Conoco at 1645 US 2 just west of Columbia Falls
Culbertson	Bruegger Bicentennial Park (city park) two blocks south of US 2 on 4th Ave E, contributions requested. Wash water available; separate drinking water spigot available. Park also has a campground with RV and tent sites.
Fort Peck	Downstream Campground (Corps of Engineers) off US 2 via MT 117, 406-526-3224
Great Falls	Cenex service station on the southeast corner of US 87 and Smelter Ave, no charge. The dump is next to the propane tank.
Great Falls	Mountain View Co-op, 1000 Smelter Ave, free
Havre	Emporium Food & Fuel on US 2 at 14th Ave
Havre	Milk River Co-op on US 2 at Montana Ave
Libby	Fireman Park campground at 905 W 9th St (US 2)
Malta	West Side Self Service on US 2

Moore	Eddie's Corner at US 87 and US 191
Plentywood	Public dump station on MT 5; east end of town just west of county fairgrounds entrance; washdown water provided but no drinking water; free
Scobey	Public dump station at Main St and Railroad Ave, one block north of only street light in town, east side of Main St, no fee
Seeley Lake	Clearwater Junction Rest Area at the junction of MT 200 and MT 83. Washdown water furnished, but no drinking water.
Seeley Lake	Lindy's across from the Post Office on MT 83, $3
Three Forks	Sinclair Station on Main St, $5 fee
Whitefish	Mike's Conoco at 6585 US 93

Nebraska

Below is a list of RV dump stations in Nebraska. Listed first are those easily accessed from Interstate highways followed by those in other locations throughout the state.

Interstate 80

Interstate 80 runs east to west for 455 miles from the Iowa state line to the Wyoming state line. Eastbound travelers should read up the chart. Westbound travelers read down the chart.

Exit(mm)	Description
432	**US 6 / NE 31 / to Gretna** Flying J Travel Plaza
430	**N 27th St / Lincoln** Leach Camper Sales, 800-289-3864, no fee. Dealer is three miles south of exit.
353	**US 81 / to York** Petro Stopping Center
332	**NE 14 / Aurora** Love's Travel Stop, free. Dump station is located on east side of pumps. Need to circle between the store and pumps to have the left side of RV next to the pit. Streeter Park (city park) in Aurora about 3 miles north of exit near junction of NE 14 and US 34. Small campground with 15 RV sites also available. Donation requested.
312	**US 34 / US 281 / to Grand Island** Bosselman Travel Center Rich and Sons Camper Sales, 308-384-2040, $3. Dealer is three miles north of exit.
305	**S Alda Rd / to Alda** TA Travel Center
190	**NE 56A / Maxwell** Fort McPherson Campground, 12568 S Valleyview Rd, 308-582-4320. Located on gravel road two miles south and one mile west of exit. $3 fee.
179	**NE 56G / North Platte** Flying J Travel Plaza

177	**US 83 / North Platte** Time Savers Texaco, 1220 S Dewey St, about one mile north of exit
164	**NE 56C / Hershey** Tomahawk Auto & Truck Plaza
126	**US 26 / NE 61 / Ogallala** TA Travel Center
59	**NE 17J / Sidney** Cabela's, 308-254-7889, free, GPS: N 41° 06.885' W 102° 57.355'

Other Locations

City or Town	Description
Beatrice	Diamond T Truck & Auto Plaza on US 77
Cambridge	Rest Area on US 6/34, east side of town on north side of road, no fee
Creighton	City park west of town center on south side of NE 59 (Main St). Free
David City	RV dump is located in the David City Park area just north of the municipal auditorium on Kansas St, east of NE 15
Fremont	Sapp Brothers Truck Stop on US 77 north of Fremont
Hastings	Adams County Fairgrounds at 947 S Baltimore Ave, just north of US 6
Holdrege	City park campground about four blocks south of US 6/34 on East Ave, south side of tracks, no fee
Humboldt	Public dump station at First St and Longbranch St, just north of city park, no charge. The city park has RV camping with hookups available for $10 per night.
Kearney	Fairgrounds at southeast corner of 39th St and Avenue N. From I-80 Exit 272, go north to 39th St and turn east to Avenue N (4 miles from exit).
McCook	Rest Area on US 6/34, east side of town on south side of road, no fee, free overnight parking
Minatare	Minatare Plaza on US 26
Neligh	City park on the southeast side of town along US 275, no fee. Follow road around park. Dump is well marked on east side of race track. Camping is also available for a nominal fee. Sites have electricity and water.
Norfolk	Ta Ha Zouka City Park, 2201 S 13th St (US 81), south of town

Ord	Bussell Park (city park) campground at N 24th St and G St, northwest side of town
Oxford	City park near the junction of US 36 and NE 46, no fee. Camping is also available.
Palmyra	Gas N Shop at US 2 and I St
Scottsbluff	Panhandle Co-op at 401 S Beltline Hwy east of NE 71
Superior	Lincoln Park on W 4th St, just north of NE 14
Tecumseh	Dump station is behind power plant at 609 Clay St, 5 blocks west of NE 50, free
Tekamah	City park on "O" St east of US 75, no fee. Campsites with electric hookups also available.
Vallentine	Northeast end of town near the ball fields at 7th St and Green St
Wayne City	Henry Victor Park on NE 15, south end of town, west side of highway, free
West Point	Neligh Park (city park), four blocks west of US 275 and one block south of fairgrounds, 402-372-2466, free. Camping is also available.

Nevada

Below is a list of RV dump stations in Nevada. Listed first are those easily accessed from Interstate highways followed by those in other locations throughout the state.

Interstate 15

Interstate 15 runs north to south for 124 miles from the Arizona state line to the California state line. Northbound travelers should read up the chart. Southbound travelers read down the chart.

Exit(mm)	Description
122	**Bus I-15 / Mesquite**
	Virgin River Casino. The dump station is in the rear of the casino RV parking area.
	Virgin River Food Mart
46	**Cheyenne Ave**
	Flying J Travel Plaza
	Hallmark Truck Center
40	**W Sahara Ave / Las Vegas**
	KOA Circus Circus, $10
33	**NV 160 / to Blue Diamond**
	Silverton Hotel Casino & RV Park, 3333 Blue Diamond Rd, 866-946-4373, $5
27	**NV 146 / to Henderson and Lake Mead**
	Vegas Valley Travel Center

Interstate 80

Interstate 80 is 411 miles long. It runs east to west from the Utah state line to the California state line. Eastbound travelers should read up the chart. Westbound travelers read down the chart.

Exit(mm)	Description
352	**US 93 / Great Basin Hwy**
	Flying J Travel Plaza
280	**NV 766 / Carlin**
	Pilot Travel Center

(258)	Rest Area
231	**NV 305 / Battle Mountain**
	Flying J Travel Plaza
(216)	Rest Area
(187)	Rest Area
176	**US 95 / Winnemucca**
	Flying J Travel Plaza
(158)	Rest Area
46	**US 95A / Fernley**
	Love's Travel Stop, 775-575-2200
(42)	Rest Area (wb)
19	**E McCarran Blvd / Sparks**
	TA Travel Center

Other Locations

City or Town	Description
Amargosa Valley	Fort Amargosa at US 95 and NV 373
Bordertown	Winners Corner on US 395 at California state line
Fallon	Churchill County Fairground south end of town, $3 donation
Gardnerville	Topaz Lodge & RV Park on US 395 just across the state line at north end of Topaz Lake, $5
Hawthorne	El Capitan Hotel & Casino on US 95. In back of casino with lots of truck and RV parking. No fee. Free overnight parking allowed.
Hawthorne	Hawthorne Shell station at 1075 US 95, dump is at the north end of property near the dumpsters
Laughlin	Harrah's convenience store at south end of Casino Dr, $5 fee
Laughlin	Riverside Casino RV Park across from Riverside Casino at north end of Casino Dr, $2 fee
Tonopah	Rest Area on US 6/95 about 10 miles northwest of town on north side of road, no fee. The dump station isn't in plain view and can be tricky to find.
Zephyr Cove	Zephyr Cove Resort RV Park on US 50 about four miles north of Stateline. $10

New Hampshire

Below is a list of RV dump stations in New Hampshire. Listed first are those easily accessed from Interstate highways followed by those in other locations throughout the state.

Interstate 89

Interstate 89 in New Hampshire runs north to south for 60 miles from the Vermont state line to Interstate 93 near Concord. Northbound travelers should read up the chart. Southbound travelers read down the chart.

Exit(mm)	Description
20	**S Main St / NH 12A / West Lebanon** Wastewater treatment plant, 130 S Main St, 603-298-5986, $5. Site is difficult to find. Road is among paved parking lots and not readily seen. From exit go north on NH 12A past two traffic lights. Look carefully on the left. The road goes off near the Electronic Super Store. Open 7 days a week; limited weekend hours.

Interstate 93

Interstate 93 in New Hampshire runs north to south for 132 miles from the Vermont state line to the Massachusetts state line. Northbound travelers should read up the chart. Southbound travelers read down the chart.

Exit(mm)	Description
34c	**NH 18 / Echo Lake** Cannon RV Park at Echo Lake, fee unknown, 7 RV sites
32	**NH 112 / Kancamagus Hwy / Lincoln** Goodie's Mobil, one mile east of exit on Kancamagus Hwy, $5 fee. Dump site with available water. Also self-serve Mobil gas, self-serve car wash and fully stocked convenience store. RV supplies and propane filling station. Open 5am to 9pm daily and to 11pm Fri & Sat.
13	**US 3 / Hall St / Concord** City of Concord wastewater treatment station, open Mon-Fri, 8:30 to 3:30, must sign in at main office and get a pass, free

Interstate 293

Interstate 293 in New Hampshire is 11 miles long. It forms an open loop around Manchester. Exit numbers are based on the consecutive numbering system.

Exit(mm)	Description
2	**NH 3A / Brown Ave / Manchester** Wastewater treatment plant, south 1/4 mile on Route 3A, first right to end, follow signs, closed weekends, no fee.

Other Locations

City or Town	Description
Keene	Wastewater treatment plant on NH 32 next to the airport, no fee. Dump is accessible from 7am to 3pm weekdays.
Lancaster	Lancaster Kwik Stop on US 2 at the Connecticut River
Merrimack	Camper's Inn (RV dealer), 35 Robert Milligan Pkwy, 603-883-1082. Dump station is in the main parking lot just to the left of the main building. Free
Merrimack	Wastewater treatment plant one mile south of Everett Turnpike Exit 10 on Daniel Webster Highway (US 3), free, no water, open 7am to 3pm daily

New Jersey

Below is a list of RV dump stations in New Jersey. Listed first are those easily accessed from Interstate highways followed by those in other locations throughout the state.

Interstate 295

Interstate 295 primarily runs north to south for 68 miles from US 1 in Trenton to the Delaware state line. Northbound travelers should read up the chart. Southbound travelers read down the chart.

Exit(mm)	Description
(3)	Welcome Center (nb)
2c	**NJ 140 / Deepwater**
	Flying J Travel Plaza

Other Locations

City or Town	Description
Belford	Middletown Sewerage Authority, open Mon-Fri 8am to 4pm, no charge. From Garden State Pkwy Exit 117, follow NJ 36 east about 5 miles past firehouse to second place where a "Main St" crosses the highway (You'll also see the Mariner Diner ahead on left). Use jughandle to cross NJ 36. Take to Center St on right then second left is Beverly into site.
Freehold	Turkey Swamp County Park south of Freehold, no fee if camping

New Mexico

Below is a list of RV dump stations in New Mexico. Listed first are those easily accessed from Interstate highways followed by those in other locations throughout the state.

Interstate 10

Interstate 10 runs east to west for 164 miles from the Texas state line to the Arizona state line. Eastbound travelers should read up the chart. Westbound travelers read down the chart.

Exit(mm)	Description
139	**NM 292 / Amador Ave / Las Cruces** TA Travel Center
20	**W Motel Dr / Lordsburg** Love's Travel Stop

Interstate 25

Interstate 25 runs north to south for 462 miles from the Colorado state line to I-10 in Las Cruces. Northbound travelers should read up the chart. Southbound travelers read down the chart.

Exit(mm)	Description
(374)	Rest Area (nb)
252	**Hagen Rd / San Felipe Pueblo** San Felipe Pueblo Travel Center
242	**NM 44 / NM 165 / US 550 / Bernalillo** Giant gas station and convenience store, free
227a	**Candelaria Rd / Albuquerque** TA Travel Center
156	**Lemitar** Roadrunner Travel Center
115	**NM 107** Santa Fe Diner & Truck Stop
75	**S Broadway St / Williamsburg / Truth or Consequences** Public dump station maintained by the Village of Williamsburg on Hyde Ave. From exit go east .6 mile to Hyde Ave and turn south. Dump is on west side of road. Open 24 hours.

Interstate 40

Interstate 40 is about 374 miles long. It runs east to west from the Texas state line to the Arizona state line. Eastbound travelers should read up the chart. Westbound travelers read down the chart.

Exit(mm)	Description
329	**US 54 / US 66**
	Ortega Shell Plaza
277	**US 84 / to Fort Sumner**
	Love's Travel Stop
194	**NM 41 / Moriarty**
	Phillip's 66, free
	Comments: The dump station is on the east side of Phillip's 66, no rinse hose. Site is not drive-thru, you may have to back up 10-15' to regain access to a drive out.
	Rip Griffin Travel Center
153	**98th St**
	Flying J Travel Plaza
39	**Refinery**
	Pilot Travel Center
(22)	Welcome Center

Other Locations

City or Town	Description
Alamogordo	Chamber of Commerce along US 54 on west side of highway midway through town. Free
Alamogordo	Timeout Travel Center at 3500 N White Sands Blvd (US 54/70)
Albuquerque	Giant Service Station at intersection of Tramway Blvd NE and Montgomery Blvd NE, no fee. Station is about four miles north of I-40 Exit 167.
Artesia	Eagle Draw City Park north of US 285 and US 82 intersection in downtown Artesia, no fee.
Belen	Giant Service Station, 19384 NM 314 (I-25 Bus), no fee, accessible from either I-25 Exit 191 (3.2 miles) or Exit 195 (2.15 miles)
Carlsbad	City of Carlsbad Lift Station. Turn east on Plaza St off Canyon St (US 62/180) at bus station, go one block, cross

	railroad tracks to dump station on left. Circle drive allows for all size rigs. No fee.
Chama	Visitor center at US 64/84 junction, no charge, fresh water spigot on side of office
Clovis	Bison RV Center, 505-762-7200, Free. Located next to Chevron station on west side, no water.
Hobbs	Harry McAdams Park on Jack Gomes Blvd (open 24 hours, $3 fee)
Hobbs	New Mexico Port of Entry on US 62 (no charge)
Los Alamos	County park east of airport on NM 502, $4 fee
Portales	Blackwater Draw Rest Area on US 70 about 7 miles northeast of town, no fee
Rio Rancho	Giant Service Station, 2101 Southern Blvd SE, no charge
Roswell	Rest area on US 285 at mile marker 149.8 about 45 miles north of Roswell and 3 miles north of US 285 and NM 20 junction. No fee.
Silver City	Gila Hot Springs near Gila Cliff Dwellings National Monument on NM 15, 38 miles north of town, no charge
Texico	Allsup's at 1400 Wheeler St (US 60/70/84)

New York

Below is a list of RV dump stations in New York. Listed first are those easily accessed from Interstate highways followed by those in other locations throughout the state.

Interstate 90

Interstate 90 runs east to west for 385 miles from the Massachusetts state line to the Pennsylvania state line. Most of it is also the New York Thruway. Exit numbers are based on the consecutive numbering system. Exit numbers *decrease* from west to east, the opposite of the normal numbering system. Eastbound travelers should read up the chart. Westbound travelers read down the chart.

Exit(mm)	Description
27	**NY 30 / Amsterdam**
	Camping World/Alpin Haus RV Super Center, 1861 NY 5S, 800-826-4413, fee unknown
41	**NY 414 / to Waterloo**
	Petro Stopping Center, 1255 Route 414, 315-220-6550, free
48a	**NY 77 / Pembroke**
	Flying J Travel Plaza
	TA Travel Center

Interstate 190

Interstate 190 is 28 miles long. It generally runs north to south from the United States/Canada border in Lewiston to I-90 in Buffalo. Exit numbers are based on the consecutive numbering system. Northbound travelers should read up the chart. Southbound travelers read down the chart.

Exit(mm)	Description
22	**US 62 / Niagara Falls Blvd**
	Junior's Fuel Plaza

Interstate 390

Interstate 390 is about 80 miles long. It generally runs north to south from Rochester to I-86 near Bath. Exit numbers are based on the consecutive numbering system. Northbound travelers should read up the chart. Southbound travelers read down the chart.

Exit(mm)	Description
5	NY 36 / Dansville
	TA Travel Center

Other Locations

City or Town	Description
Albany	Wastewater treatment plant, 1 Canal Rd, no water, free. Can be accessed from I-787 Exit 6.
Avon	Municipal waste treatment plant off US 20, west of roundabout in center of town at bottom of hill and before river, dump site is a manhole cover with handle, contributions accepted
Catskill	Brookside Campground, 4952 Route 32, 800-390-4412, $20. From I-87 Exit 20, go north about 9 miles on NY Route 32.
Durham	The Milk Run Truck Stop at 3552 NY 145
Hawthorne	Westchester dump station just off NY 9A at intersection with NY 141, easy drive through, no fee
Huntington	Wastewater treatment facility on Creek Rd. From I-495 Exit 49N, follow NY 110 (New York Ave) north through town. About one mile north of Main St, turn left on Creek Rd. Facility is on the right, no fee.
Johnstown	Wastewater treatment plant on Union Ave, $5. From I-90 Exit 28 follow NY 30A north 4 miles to Union Ave and turn west. Follow Union Ave about one mile to plant. From NY 30A, Union Ave goes down and around a sharp bend and crosses a narrow bridge. Open 8am to 3pm weekdays.
Old Bethpage	Battle Row Campground (county park) on Claremont Rd, 516-572-8690 $5 fee for non-campers. From Long Island Expy, take the Round Swamp Rd exit and follow south to Sweethollow Rd and turn left. Follow this road to Claremont Rd and turn right. Campground is closed Nov thru Mar.

Palmyra	Palmyra waste plant on NY 31 between fire station and supermarket, no fee is charged
Rome	Erie Canal Village on the west side of town just south of the NY 69 and NY 46 intersection at the end of the Erie Canal Village parking lot. Free
Schenectady	City wastewater treatment plant on Anthony St. From I-890 take the General Electric plant ext and follow signs for Erie Blvd. Follow for about one mile and turn right onto Maxon Rd Extension. Follow to Van Vranken Ave and bare left. Anthony St is the next left turn. Treatment plant is at end of street. If you find the gate closed it is okay to open and drive in, just close the gate again.

North Carolina

Below is a list of RV dump stations in North Carolina. Listed first are those easily accessed from Interstate highways followed by those in other locations throughout the state.

Interstate 40

Interstate 40 runs east to west for 420 miles from Wilmington to the Tennessee state line. Part of it is also I-85. Eastbound travelers should read up the chart. Westbound travelers read down the chart.

Exit(mm)	Description
150	**Jimmie Kerr Rd / Haw River**
	Flying J Travel Plaza

Interstate 85

Interstate 85 runs north to south for 234 miles from the Virginia state line to the South Carolina state line. Part of it is shared with I-40. Northbound travelers should read up the chart. Southbound travelers read down the chart.

Exit(mm)	Description
150	**Jimmie Kerr Rd / Haw River**
	Flying J Travel Plaza
5	**Dixon School Rd**
	Kings Mountain Truck Plaza

Interstate 95

Interstate 95 is 182 miles long. It runs north to south from the Virginia state line to the South Carolina state line. Northbound travelers should read up the chart. Southbound travelers read down the chart.

Exit(mm)	Description
106	**Kenly**
	TA Travel Center
75	**Jonesboro Rd**
	Sadler Travel Plaza

1	US 301
	Porky's Truck Stop

Interstate 440

Interstate 440 in North Carolina is a 16-mile route around Raleigh. Exit numbering begins at Jones Franklin Rd and increases in a clockwise direction.

Exit(mm)	Description
13b	**US 64 / US 264 / New Bern Ave / Raleigh**
	College Park RV, 4208 New Bern Ave, 919-231-8710, $15 fee. Dump station is behind the dealership.

Other Locations

City or Town	Description
Brevard	Davidson River Campground (Pisgah National Forest), $3 fee, on US 276 about 4 miles north of town
Buxton	Cape Hatteras National Seashore campground. Go 1/2 mile past the parking lot for the lighthouse toward the campground. The dump station is on the left.
Elizabeth City	Quality Inn at 522 S Hughes Blvd (US 17)
Harrisburg	Politis Texaco at 4025 NC Hwy 49
Manteo	Oregon Inlet Fishing Center, 800-272-5199, free. Located 8 miles south of Whalebone Junction on NC 12 at the north end of the Oregon Inlet Bridge in Cape Hatteras National Seashore. Upon entering Oregon Inlet Fishing Center, take the first left to the parking area. The dump station will be located on the left.
Manteo	Rest area/welcome center on US 64 just before entering the Outer Banks, free
New Bern	Flanners Beach/Neuse River Campground in Croatan National Forest about ten miles south of town off US 70, $5
Rocky Point	Rocky Point Campground & Shooters World at 14565 Ashton Rd, $5 fee. Campground is 7 miles northwest of I-40 Exit 408 via US 117 and Ashton Rd.
Rural Hall	Bill Plemmons RV World, 800-732-0507, $5. Dealer is on University Pkwy about three miles north of US 52 Exit 115.

North Dakota

Below is a list of RV dump stations in North Dakota. Listed first are those easily accessed from Interstate highways followed by those in other locations throughout the state.

Interstate 29

I-29 runs north to south for 218 miles from the United States/Canada border to the South Dakota state line. Northbound travelers should read up the chart. Southbound travelers read down the chart.

Exit(mm)	Description
141	**US 2 / Gateway Dr / Grand Forks**
	E-Z Stop Truck Stop, no fee
	StaMart Travel Plaza
138	**32nd Ave / Grand Forks**
	Big Sioux Travel Plaza
66	**12th Ave N / Fargo**
	StaMart Travel Center at 3500 12th Ave N, no fee, easy access
62	**32nd Ave / Fargo**
	Flying J Travel Plaza

Interstate 94

Interstate 94 runs east to west for 352 miles from the Minnesota state line to the Montana state line. Eastbound travelers should read up the chart. Westbound travelers read down the chart.

Exit(mm)	Description
348	**45th St / Fargo**
	Petro Stopping Center
157	**Divide Ave / Bismarck**
	Cenex station, south of exit
	Comments: Dump is next to car wash, across from Miracle Mart supermarket, no fee, propane is also available
	Conoco/MVP, north of exit
	Comments: Dump is on south side of building, no fee

147	**ND 25 / Mandan**
	Freeway 147 Truck Stop
61	**ND 22 / Dickinson**
	The General Store

Other Locations

City or Town	Description
Devil's Lake	Cenex C-Store at US 2 and ND 19
Hazen	Car wash along ND 200, east side of town, no fee
Minot	Behm's Truck Stop at 3800 US 2/52, free
Minot	Corner Express Amoco, 3630 S Broadway (US 83), free
Minot	Dawn to Dusk Amoco, 7141 E Burdick Expy, free
Minot	Econo Stop at US 2/52 Bypass and US 83, free
Minot	North Central Service Heating & Cooling, 515 31st Ave SW, free
Rugby	Cenex Truck Plaza near junction of ND 3 and US 2
Rugby	Hi-Way MVP Station at 209 US 2
Stanley	City park on Main St about 3/4 mile north of US 2, just north of the railroad overpass. Camping is also available for free up to 4 days or a donation.
Tioga	City park at 4th St and Gilbertson NE
Valley City	City park campground at 600 E Main St (I-94 Bus), free if camping, accessible from I-94 Exit 290 (2 miles), Exit 292 (1.7 miles), Exit 294 (1.6 miles)
Velva	Cenex Station right off US 52 in town - open during summer travel season
Williston	OK Conoco North on US 2/85

Ohio

Below is a list of RV dump stations in Ohio. Listed first are those easily accessed from Interstate highways followed by those in other locations throughout the state.

Interstate 70

Interstate 70 runs east to west for 226 miles from the West Virginia state line to the Indiana state line. Eastbound travelers should read up the chart. Westbound travelers read down the chart.

Exit(mm)	Description
160	OH 797 / Airport
	Love's Travel Stop
122	OH 158 / Kirkersville
	Flying J Travel Plaza

Interstate 71

Interstate 71 runs north to south for 248 miles from I-90 in Cleveland to the Kentucky state line. Northbound travelers should read up the chart. Southbound travelers read down the chart.

Exit(mm)	Description
218	OH 18 / Medina Rd / Medina
	Avalon RV Center, 1604 Medina Rd, Medina OH 44256, 800-860-7728, Free
	Comments: Family owned and operated since 1968. Large selection of RVs, Boats, Parts & Accessories. RVIA certified technicians and 20 service bays. A proud REDEX dealer.
209	US 224 / I-76 / to Akron
	TA Travel Center
140	OH 61 / Mount Gilead
	Pilot Travel Center
131	US 36 / OH 37
	Flying J Travel Plaza
69	OH 41 / OH 734 / Jeffersonville
	Flying J Travel Plaza

Interstate 75

Interstate 75 runs north to south for 211 miles from the Michigan state line to the Kentucky state line. Northbound travelers should read up the chart. Southbound travelers read down the chart.

Exit(mm)	Description
135	**OH 696 / Beaverdam / to US 30** Flying J Travel Plaza Pilot Travel Center
36	**OH 123 / Franklin** Shell gas station next to Pilot Travel Center

Interstate 76

Interstate 76 runs east to west for 82 miles from the Pennsylvania state line to I-71 south of Medina. Part of it is also the Ohio Turnpike. Eastbound travelers should read up the chart. Westbound travelers read down the chart.

Exit(mm)	Description
1	**I-71 / US 224** TA Travel Center

Interstate 77

Interstate 77 in Ohio is 160 miles long. It runs north to south from I-90 in Cleveland to the West Virginia state line. Northbound travelers should read up the chart. Southbound travelers read down the chart.

Exit(mm)	Description
111	**Portage St NW / North Canton** Beggs RV Center, 6075 Dressler Rd NW, 800-837-8100, fee charged

Interstate 80

I-80 runs east to west for 237 miles from the Pennsylvania state line to the Indiana state line. Portions are also I-90 and the Ohio Turnpike.

Eastbound travelers should read up the chart. Westbound travelers read down the chart.

Exit(mm)	Description
234	**US 62 / OH 7 / N Main St / Hubbard**
	Flying J Travel Plaza
223	**OH 46 / to Niles**
	TA Travel Center
(197)	Rest Area
180	**OH 8**
	Kamper City, 5549 Akron-Cleveland Rd, 330-650-1491, $10
	Comments: From exit, follow OH 8 south to OH 303/Akron-Cleveland Rd exit. Continue straight through the light about one mile. Kamper City is on the left.
(139)	Rest Area
(77)	Rest Area
34	**OH 108 / to Wauseon**
	Fulton County Fairgrounds, $7 fee. Dump station is in the southwest part of fairground. Pay the care takers at the mobile home in park. Overnight camping is also available for $15 per night.
(21)	Rest Area (wb)

Interstate 90

Interstate 90 runs east to west for 245 miles from the Pennsylvania state line to the Indiana state line. Part of it is also I-80 and the Ohio Turnpike. Eastbound travelers should read up the chart. Westbound travelers read down the chart.

Exit(mm)	Description
223	**OH 45 / to Ashtabula**
	Flying J Travel Plaza
(139)	Rest Area
(77)	Rest Area
34	**OH 108 / to Wauseon**
	Fulton County Fairgrounds, $7 fee. Dump station is in the southwest part of fairground. Pay the care takers at the mobile home in park. Overnight camping is also available for $15 per night.
(21)	Rest Area (wb)

Interstate 280

Interstate 280 is 12 miles long. It connects I-80/90 with I-75 in Toledo.

Exit(mm)	Description
1b	Bahnsen Dr
	Flying J Travel Plaza

Other Locations

City or Town	Description
Akron	Portage Lakes State Park, 330-644-2220. Free for registered campers, $10 fee if not camping. Park is 7 miles west of I-77 Exit 133. From exit turn right on Lauby Rd; turn left of Greensburg Rd; go through Greensburg to E Nimisila Rd and turn left. Nimisila Rd will dead-end at Christman Rd. The campground is directly across Nimisila Rd at this intersection. The dump station is in the camping area on Nimisila Reservoir.
Bellevue	Lazy J Campground on US 20 about three miles west of town, $6
Dalton	Citgo Bell Store at northeast corner of US 30 and OH 94, north side of parking lot, $5 or free with fuel purchase
Deersville	Tappan Lake Park, 1 1/2 miles north of town
Dover	Tuscarawas County Fairgrounds at 259 S Tuscarawas Ave
Galion	Craig Smith RV Center, 866-462-1746, Free
Mineral City	Atwood Lake Park, 9 miles southeast of town on Lakeview Rd (CR 114)
Sandusky	Gatsby Transportation Inc, 419-626-8444, on US 6 about one mile east of OH 2 and US 6 interchange, next to Coronado Motel, $10 fee
Sylvania	All American Coach Co., 419-885-4601, $8.50. Dealership is one mile east of US 23.
Tiffin	Dump station is just off OH 53 on the north side of town, no fee, site name is unknown
Van Wert	Van Wert County Fairgrounds at 1055 S Washington St (US 127)

Oklahoma

Below is a list of RV dump stations in Oklahoma. Listed first are those easily accessed from Interstate highways followed by those in other locations throughout the state.

Interstate 35

Interstate 35 runs north to south for 236 miles from the Kansas state line to the Texas state line. Portions are also shared with I-40 and I-44. Northbound travelers should read up the chart. Southbound travelers read down the chart.

Exit(mm)	Description
(225)	Welcome Center (sb) / Rest Area (nb)
185	**US 77 / Perry**
	Sooner's Corner Texaco
137	**NE 122nd St**
	Flying J Travel Plaza
	Love's Travel Stop
(59)	Rest Area

Interstate 40

Interstate 40 runs east to west for 331 miles from the Arkansas state line to the Texas state line. Part of it is shared with I-35. Eastbound travelers should read up the chart. Westbound travelers read down the chart.

Exit(mm)	Description
(316)	Rest Area (eb)
(314)	Welcome Center (wb)
264b	**US 69 / to Eufaula**
	Flying J Travel Plaza
(197)	Rest Area
142	**Council Rd**
	TA Travel Center
140	**Morgan Rd**
	Flying J Travel Plaza
	Pilot Travel Center

101	US 281 / OK 8 / to Hinton
	Hinton Travel Plaza
20	US 283 / Sayre
	Flying J Travel Plaza
(10)	Welcome Center (eb) / Rest Area (wb)
7	OK 30 / Erick
	Texaco Log Cabin
1	Texola
	Double D Fuel Stop

Interstate 44

Interstate 44 runs east to west for about 329 miles from the Missouri state line to the Texas state line. Part of it is shared with I-35. Much of I-44 is part of Oklahoma's toll-highway system. Eastbound travelers should read up the chart. Westbound travelers read down the chart.

Exit(mm)	Description
248	OK 66 / OK 266
	Dave's Claremore RV, 918-341-0114, Free. Dealer is three miles south of Claremore on Hwy 66. Dump station is in front of dealership and is well marked.
236a	129th E Ave
	Flying J Travel Plaza
137	NE 122nd St
	Flying J Travel Plaza
	Love's Travel Stop

Interstate 244

Interstate 244 is 15 miles long. It forms a partial loop around Tulsa. Exit numbering begins at West 51st Ave and increases in a clockwise direction.

Exit(mm)	Description
15	129th E Ave
	Flying J Travel Plaza

Other Locations

City or Town	Description
Boise City	Love's Travel Stop at US 287 and US 56
Checotah	Flying J Travel Plaza at US 69 and US 266
Chouteau	Love's Travel Stop at US 412 and US 69
Colbert	Sherrard RV & KOA, 580-296-2485, $1
Cromwell	Four Winds Ranch, 405-944-1180, $5 for non-guests, free for overnight guests
Eufaula	Love's Travel Stop on US 69
Hooker	Love's Travel Stop at US 54 and US 64
Pauls Valley	Longmire City Lake about 14 miles east of town off OK 19
Pauls Valley	Pauls Valley City Lake about two miles northeast of town off OK 19
Woodward	Kevin's Corner Texaco at 3710 US 183

Oregon

Below is a list of RV dump stations in Oregon. Listed first are those easily accessed from Interstate highways followed by those in other locations throughout the state.

Interstate 5

Interstate 5 runs north to south for 308 miles from the Washington state line to the California state line. Northbound travelers should read up the chart. Southbound travelers read down the chart.

Exit(mm)	Description
307	**OR 99E / Marine Dr** Jubitz Travel Center
238	**OR 99E / Old Salem Rd** McKay Truck and RV Center, 6225 Old Salem Rd NE, 541-928-3331, one mile west of exit, easy on and off, no hassle turnaround, $5 fee, open 24 hours
234	**Knox Butte Rd / Albany** Knox Butte RV Park, $5 fee, 541-928-9033 *Comments*: Southbound travelers use Exit 234a
199	**Coburg** TA Travel Center
136	**W Central Ave / Sutherlin** McGuffies BP Gas Station ($3 fee)
129	**OR 99 / Del Rio Rd** Kamper Korner RV Center, 541-673-1258, $3. From exit go north on Hwy 99 1 1/2 miles to dealership.
123	**Heritage Way / SW Portland Ave / Roseburg** Douglas County Fairgrounds ($3 fee)
119	**OR 99 / Roseburg** Love's Travel Stop
99	**Main St / Canyonville** Stanton County Park ($3 fee)
86	**Quines Creek Rd** Meadow Wood RV Park, 869 Autumn Ln, 800-606-1274, $5 *Comments*: From southbound I-5 take Exit 86, go east over Interstate to dead end, right 3 miles to Barton Rd, left 500 feet to Autumn Ln, right one mile to park office.

83	**Barton Rd**
	Meadow Wood RV Park, 869 Autumn Ln, 800-606-1274, $5
	Comments: From northbound I-5 take Exit 83, right 500
	feet to Autumn Ln, right one mile to park office.
58	**OR 99 / NE 6th St / Grants Pass**
	76 service station, 1995 NE 6th St, 541-474-9344, free
45b	**Valley of the Rogue State Park**
	Rest Area in Valley of the Rogue State Park
14	**OR 66 / Ashland St / Ashland**
	Shell service station, $3 fee or free with fuel purchase. Water
	available for washing tanks.

Interstate 84

I-84 runs east to west for approximately 378 miles from the Idaho state line to I-5 in Portland. Eastbound travelers should read up the chart. Westbound travelers read down the chart.

Exit(mm)	Description
376	**US 30 / Idaho Ave / Ontario**
	Pilot Travel Center
374	**OR 201 / US 30**
	Rest Area in Ontario State Park
304	**OR 7 / Baker**
	Baker Truck Corral
	Jackson's Food Mart
(269)	Rest Area
228	**Deadman Pass**
	Rest Area
(73)	Rest Area (eb)
63	**N 2nd St / Hood River**
	Hood River Waste Treatment Plant at 818 Riverside Dr
17	**Marine Dr / Troutdale**
	Flying J Travel Plaza, 400 NW Frontage Rd, 503-665-7741,
	GPS: N 45° 32.370' W 122° 23.944'

Interstate 205

Interstate 205 is a 37-mile route in Oregon and Washington. It forms an open loop around the Portland and Vancouver areas.

Exit(mm)	Description
9	OR 99E / McLoughlin Ave / Oregon City
	Clackamette RV Park (city park)

Other Locations

City or Town	Description
Bandon	Bullards Beach State Park on US 101 about two miles north of town
Bend	Expressway Market on Reed Market Rd east of US 97 at 15th St, $5 fee. Non-potable water available.
Bend	Texaco at 3rd St (US 97) and Revere Ave - $3 with fuel purchase
Brookings	Rest Area on US 101 about 2 miles north of Brookings at Harris Beach State Park
Burns	Rest Area on US 20 about 18 miles west of Burns
Canby	Professional Car Wash & Laundromat on S Birch St between Taco Bell and Burgerville, south side of OR 99E. $5 fee. Dump station is in back of laundromat by the car wash.
Coos Bay	Dump station is on US 101 in center of town ($1 honor pay)
Cottage Grove	Water Treatment Plant at 1800 N Douglas - open Mon thru Fri 9 to 3 (closed noon to 1), $4 fee
Durham	Durham Wastewater Treatment Plant at 16580 SW 85th Ave, free
Eugene	Wastewater Treatment Plant on River Ave off the Beltline Road
Florence	Harbor Vista County Park about 3 miles north of town via US 101, 35th St, and N Rhododendron Dr, $3 fee
Florence	Jessie M. Honeyman State Park, on road to camping area before registration booth.
Florence	Rest Area on US 101 about 14 miles north of Florence at C.G. Washburne State Park
Garibaldi	Barview Jetty Park on US 101 about 1 mile north of Garibaldi

Hermiston	The Station at US 395 and W Catherine Ave, no fee, dump is near the porta potty
Hillsboro	Olinger Travel Homes at 230th and TV Hwy (6503 SE Alexander St)
Hillsboro	Rock Creek Wastewater Treatment Plant at 3125 SE River Rd
Irrigon	Brown's Auto & Truck Stop on US 730 about 6 miles north of I-84 Exit 168
Island City	C&M Country Store at 10102 N Hwy 82
John Day	Rest Area on US 26 about 4 miles west of John Day at Clyde Holiday State Park
Klamath Falls	Airport RV Storage, 2931 Bristal Ave, 541-273-0142, $5 or free to renters.
Klamath Falls	Klamath County Fairgrounds at 3531 S 6th St (OR 39) - $3 fee
Klamath Falls	Moore Park Marina on Lakeshore Dr by restrooms - free
Klamath Falls	Suburban Self Storage at 3939 Hilyard Ave - from US 97 travel east of OR 39 to Summers Ln. Turn south and follow to Hilyard Ave - $3 fee
La Pine	Gordy's Truck Stop on east side of US 97 about three miles north of town, $6
Lebanon	River Park on Grant St east of US 20. Go about one mile east on Grant St from downtown. Just before the bridge crossing turn left into the city park and left into campground ($10 per night, no hookups). $3 fee to use dump. A new campground and dump station will replace the existing facility sometime in 2005. The new facility will be at Gill's Landing Park, which is directly across the street from River Park.
Madras	Public dump station adjacent to City Public Works; west on B St from US97/US 26 at north end of town. $3 donation requested
McMinnville	Water Reclamation Facility at 3500 Clearwater Dr
Mill City	Riverbend Campground on OR 22, $3 fee
Newport	Chamber of Commerce at US 101 and Fall St, east side of highway, free, non-potable water. Easy access from US 101. Turn east on Abby St (Apple Peddler Restaurant on east corner), make a left on 9th St and left on Fall St.
Newport	In parking lot south of Rogue Brewery, which is at the

	South Beach Marina underneath the south end of Yaquina Bay Bridge, no fee
Newport	Public dump station 1/2 block east of US 101 on 9th St, free
Newport	South Beach State Park about 1 1/4 miles south of Yaquina Bridge on US 101, donations accepted.
Ontario	Malheur County Fairgrounds at 795 NW 9th St
Pacific City	Webb Park off Cape Kiwanda Dr about 1 mile north of Pacific City
Pendleton	In parking lot of train depot museum on Frazier Street between SE 2nd & SE 3rd, easy in and out, free, donations welcomed but not required
Prineville	Crook County Chamber of Commerce at 390 NE Fairview St off US 26
Rainier	Wastewater treatment plant on US 30 next to city park, northwest end of town, no fee, difficult to use if towing a "toad"
Reedsport	Oregon Dunes NRA Visitor Center at north end of town at the junction of US 101 and OR 38, $3 fee.
Reedsport	Rest Area on US 101 about 8 miles south of Reedsport at William Tugman State Park
Saint Helens	Mobile One Stop/Union 76 gas station on US 30, south end of town, between Burgerville and Safeway (grocery store), $1.50 fee
Scappoose	Jackpot/Exxon Station on US 30, $3
Sisters	City park on US 20 north of town, no fee. Camping is also available.
Sweet Home	Sweet Home RV Center, 4691 US 20, 541-367-4293, $5
Tillamook	Trask Park on Trask River Rd about 14 miles east of Tillamook
Toledo	A public dump station is located at the Georgia Pacific Paper Mill off US 20 in Toledo. It is by Gate 3 and contractor parking lot. A fee of .25 is charged for water.
Unity	Rest Area on OR 245 at Unity Lake State Park
Vernonia	Anderson Park (city park), 450 Jefferson Ave, 503-429-2531, $5. 19 RV sites with full hookups also available.
Parkdale	Toll Bridge County Park on OR 35 east of Parkdale
Winchester Bay	Salmon Harbor County Park on Oak Rock Rd between boat basins. From US 101, turn right onto 9th St, then onto Oak Rock Rd. Dump is free if camping.
Woodburn	Waste Treatment Plant at 2815 Molalla Rd (OR 211)

Pennsylvania

Below is a list of RV dump stations in Pennsylvania. Listed first are those easily accessed from Interstate highways followed by those in other locations throughout the state.

Interstate 70

I-70 runs east to west for about 173 miles from the Maryland state line to the West Virginia state line. Portions are also shared with I-76, I-79, and the Pennsylvania Turnpike. Eastbound travelers should read up the chart. Westbound travelers read down the chart.

Exit(mm)	Description
49	**Smithton**
	Penn Station Travel Plaza
6	**US 40 / Claysville**
	Petro Stopping Center

Interstate 76

Interstate 76 runs east to west for about 350 miles from the New Jersey state line to the Ohio state line. Nearly all of I-76 is also the Pennsylvania Turnpike. Part of the Interstate is also shared with I-70. Eastbound travelers should read up the chart. Westbound travelers read down the chart.

Exit(mm)	Description
350	**Packer Ave / 7th St**
	Walt Whitman Truck Stop
(325)	Rest Area (eb)
(259)	Rest Area (wb)
(172)	Rest Area

Interstate 78

Interstate 78 in Pennsylvania runs east to west for about 77 miles from the New Jersey state line to Interstate 81 Exit 89 near Jonestown.

Exit(mm)	Description
26b	**PA 61 N / Hamburg**
	Cabela's, 610-929-7000, free, GPS: N 40° 33.481' W 76° 00.188'

Interstate 80

Interstate 80 runs east to west for 311 miles from the New Jersey state line to the Ohio state line. Eastbound travelers should read up the chart. Westbound travelers read down the chart.

Exit(mm)	Description
215	**PA 254 / Limestoneville**
	Petro Stopping Center
173	**PA 64 / Lamar / to Mill Hall**
	Flying J Travel Plaza, 570-726-4080
78	**PA 36 / Brookville**
	Flying J Travel Plaza
	TA Travel Center

Interstate 81

Interstate 81 runs north to south 233 miles from the New York state line to the Maryland state line. Northbound travelers should read up the chart. Southbound travelers read down the chart.

Exit(mm)	Description
219	**PA 848 / to Gibson**
	Flying J Travel Plaza
178b	**Avoca / to US 11**
	Petro Stopping Center
52	**US 11**
	Flying J Travel Plaza

Interstate 90

Interstate 90 runs east to west for 46 miles from the New York state line to the Ohio state line. Eastbound travelers should read up the chart. Westbound travelers read down the chart.

Exit(mm)	Description
35	PA 531 / to Harborcreek
	TA Travel Center

Interstate 95

Interstate 95 runs north to south for 51 miles from the New Jersey state line to the Delaware state line. Northbound travelers should read up the chart. Southbound travelers read down the chart.

Exit(mm)	Description
19	I-76 / to Oregon Ave
	Walt Whitman Truck Stop

Interstate 99

Interstate 99 is 53 miles long. It runs north to south between Bald Eagle and I-70/I-76/PA Turnpike near Bedford. Northbound travelers should read up the chart. Southbound travelers read down the chart.

Exit(mm)	Description
23	PA 36 / PA 164 / Roaring Spring
	CoGo's Travel Center

Interstate 276

Interstate 276 near Philadelphia is about 33 miles long. It runs east to west from the New Jersey state line to I-76. It is also part of the Pennsylvania Turnpike. Eastbound travelers should read up the chart. Westbound travelers read down the chart.

Exit(mm)	Description
(352)	Welcome Center (wb) / Rest Area (eb)

Interstate 476

Interstate 476 is a 131-mile route running north to south from Scranton to I-95 in Woodlyn. Much of it is part of Pennsylvania's toll highway system. Northbound travelers should read up the chart. Southbound travelers read down the chart.

Exit(mm)	Description
(56)	Lehigh Valley Service Plaza

Other Locations

City or Town	Description
Dallas	Bryant's RV Showcase on PA 415, $5 fee, drop box for fee after hours
Ephrata	222 Travel Plaza at US 222 and US 322
Milroy	Unimart on US 322
Uniontown	Wastewater treatment plant at 90 Romeo Ln near junction of US 119 and PA 51, no fee

Rhode Island

Below is a list of RV dump stations easily accessed from Interstate highways in Rhode Island.

Interstate 95

Interstate 95 runs north to south for 43 miles from the Massachusetts state line to the Connecticut state line. Exit numbers are based on the consecutive numbering system. Northbound travelers should read up the chart. Southbound travelers read down the chart.

Exit(mm)	Description
8	RI 2 / Quaker Ln / East Greenwich
	Arlington RV (Mon thru Sat, 8am to 5pm), $5 fee

South Carolina

Below is a list of RV dump stations in South Carolina. Listed first are those easily accessed from Interstate highways followed by those in other locations throughout the state.

Interstate 20

Interstate 20 runs east to west for 142 miles from I-95 near Florence to the Georgia state line. Eastbound travelers should read up the chart. Westbound travelers read down the chart.

Exit(mm)	Description
70	US 321 / Fairfield Rd
	Flying J Travel Plaza

Interstate 26

Interstate 26 in South Carolina is an east-west route that is 221 miles long. It runs from US 17 in Charleston to the North Carolina state line. Eastbound travelers should read up the chart. Westbound travelers read down the chart.

Exit(mm)	Description
205a	US 78 / University Blvd
	KOA campground one mile west of exit on US 78, $10

Interstate 77

Interstate 77 runs north to south for 91 miles from the North Carolina state line to I-26 in Columbia. Northbound travelers should read up the chart. Southbound travelers read down the chart.

Exit(mm)	Description
34	SC 34 / Ridgeway
	Ridgeway Campground east of exit, $7

Interstate 85

Interstate 85 runs north to south for 106 miles from the North Carolina state line to the Georgia state line. Northbound travelers should read up the chart. Southbound travelers read down the chart.

Exit(mm)	Description
102	SC 198 / to Earl
	Flying J Travel Plaza

Interstate 95

Interstate 95 runs north to south for 198 miles from the North Carolina state line to the Georgia state line. Northbound travelers should read up the chart. Southbound travelers read down the chart.

Exit(mm)	Description
1	US 301
	Porky's Truck Stop
181	SC 38 / Oak Grove
	Flying J Travel Plaza
	Wilco Travel Plaza
169	TV Rd / to Florence
	Petro Stopping Center
119	SC 261 / Manning
	TA Travel Center

Other Locations

City or Town	Description
Goose Creek	Lower Berkeley Wastewater Treatment Plant at 2111 Red Bank Rd
Greenville	Paris Mountain State Park, $6. The park is reached through a residential area but is clearly marked. Pay when entering the park. Mark on the envelope "dumping only."
Lexington	Edmund RV Park, 5920 Edmund Hwy, 803-955-4010, $5 fee. From I-20 Exit 55 follow SC 6 south for 7 miles. From I-26 Exit 113 follow SC 302 south for about 9 miles.
Seneca	High Falls County Park about 13 miles north of town via SC 130 and SC 183
Seneca	South Cove County Park about 4 miles north of Seneca via SC 28 and SC 188
Westminster	Chau Ram County Park 3 miles west of town on US 76

South Dakota

Below is a list of RV dump stations in South Dakota. Listed first are those easily accessed from Interstate highways followed by those in other locations throughout the state.

Interstate 29

Interstate 29 runs north to south for 253 miles from the North Dakota state line to the Iowa state line. Northbound travelers should read up the chart. Southbound travelers read down the chart.

Exit(mm)	Description
213	**SD 15 / to Wilmot**
	Rest Area east of exit
177	**US 212 / Watertown**
	Stone's Truck Stop
(161)	Rest Area
121	**CR B / 223rd St**
	Rest Area east of exit
83	**SD 38 / W 60th St / Sioux Falls**
	Flying J Travel Plaza
26	**SD 50 / Vermillion**
	Welcome Center east of exit

Interstate 90

Interstate 90 runs east to west for 413 miles from the Minnesota state line to the Wyoming state line. Eastbound travelers should read up the chart. Westbound travelers read down the chart.

Exit(mm)	Description
(412)	Welcome Center (wb)
(363)	Rest Area
332	**SD 37 / Mitchell**
	Cabela's, 605-996-0337, free, GPS: N 43° 41.441' W 98° 01.035'
(302)	Rest Area (wb)
(301)	Rest Area (eb)
(264)	Rest Area

(221)	Rest Area (wb)
(218)	Rest Area (eb)
(167)	Rest Area (wb)
(165)	Rest Area (eb)
(100)	Rest Area
66	**Box Elder**
	Flying J Travel Plaza
61	**Elk Vale Rd**
	Flying J Travel Plaza
58	**N Haines Ave**
	Conoco
55	**Deadwood Ave**
	Windmill Truck Stop
(42)	Rest Area
30	**SD 34 / US 14A / Sturgis**
	Cenex Station
(1)	Welcome Center (eb)

Other Locations

City or Town	Description
Armour	Lion's Park on east side of US 281 in town, donations accepted
Belle Fourche	Chamber of Commerce at 415 5th Ave (US 85)
Brookings	Sexauer Park at Western Ave and 8th St. This city park also has 13 campsites with electric hookups.
Burke	Public dump station behind Pump & Stuff convenience store on US 18 in town, no fee.
Deadwood	Ken's Camper Sales on Hwy 14A between Deadwood and Lead
Flandreau	Flandreau City Park one mile east of town, camping for less than $10 per day. Watch your height when entering the gate. There is a bypass available to avoid the gate.
Ipswich	Collier's Park at US 12 and 9th St, no charge
Pierre	Griffin City Park on Missouri Ave along riverfront about 3 blocks south of Dakota Ave. Free. 15 RV sites with hookups also available.
Sturgis	City Park on Lazelle St (SD 34) at Nellie St
Wolsey	281 Travel Center on US 14/281 at mile marker 331

Tennessee

Below is a list of RV dump stations in Tennessee. Listed first are those easily accessed from Interstate highways followed by those in other locations throughout the state.

Interstate 40

I-40 runs east to west for about 455 miles from the North Carolina state line to the Arkansas state line. Portions are also shared with I-24 and I-75. Eastbound travelers should read up the chart. Westbound travelers read down the chart.

Exit(mm)	Description
369	**Watt Rd**
	Flying J Travel Plaza
	Petro Stopping Center, 865-693-6542. Dump station is at left front side of parking lot. Free
288	**TN 111 / Cookeville**
	Middle Tennessee Auto & Truck Plaza
238	**US 231 / Lebanon**
	Pilot Travel Center
182	**TN 96 / to Dickson**
	Flying J Travel Plaza
172	**TN 46 / to Dickson**
	Pilot Travel Center
126	**US 641 / TN 69 / to Camden**
	North Forty Truck Stop
87	**US 70 / US 412 / Jackson**
	Love's Travel Stop

Interstate 75

Interstate 75 in Tennessee runs north to south for 162 miles from the Kentucky state line to the Georgia state line. Portions are shared with I-

640 and I-40. Northbound travelers should read up the chart. Southbound travelers read down the chart.

Exit(mm)	Description
369	**Watt Rd** Flying J Travel Plaza Petro Stopping Center, 865-693-6542. Dump station is at left front side of parking lot. Free

Interstate 81

Interstate 81 runs north to south for 76 miles from the Virginia state line to I-40 near Dandridge. Northbound travelers should read up the chart. Southbound travelers read down the chart.

Exit(mm)	Description
4	**TN 341 / White Pine** Pilot Travel Center

Other Locations

City or Town	Description
Chattanooga	Chester Frost Park (county park) off Hixson Pike (TN 319) about 5 miles north of TN 153. There are two dump stations, one is right off the main drive and is somewhat crowded. The other is more distant, sheltered, and easily accessible. No fee is charged.
Kingsport	Wastewater Treatment Plant at 620 W Industry Dr (free)
Knoxville	Southlake RV Park, 3730 Maryville Pike (TN 33), 865-573-1837, $5 fee, Good Sam Park
Tazewell	Exxon station at 1446 N Broad St
Tellico Plains	KOA, 7310 Hwy 360, 423-253-2447, $10

Texas

Below is a list of RV dump stations in Texas. Listed first are those easily accessed from Interstate highways followed by those in other locations throughout the state.

Interstate 10

Interstate 10 runs east to west for 881 miles from the Louisiana state line to the New Mexico state line. Part of it is shared with I-35. Eastbound travelers should read up the chart. Westbound travelers read down the chart.

Exit(mm)	Description
873	**TX 62 / TX 73 / to Bridge City**
	Flying J Travel Plaza
(590)	Rest Area
583	**Foster Rd**
	Flying J Travel Plaza
	TA Travel Center
(514)	Rest Area
(394)	Rest Area
372	**Taylor Box Rd**
	Circle Bar Auto & Truck Plaza
212	**TX 17 / FM 2448 / to Pecos**
	I-10 Fina
87	**FM 34**
	Tiger Travel Plaza
0	**FM 1905 / Anthony**
	Flying J Travel Plaza
	Pilot Travel Center

Interstate 20

Interstate 20 runs east to west for 636 miles from the Louisiana state line to I-10 near Kent. Eastbound travelers should read up the chart. Westbound travelers read down the chart.

Exit(mm)	Description
503	**Wilson Rd**
	Rip Griffin Travel Center

472	**Bonnie View Rd**
	Flying J Travel Plaza
	TA Travel Center
466	**S Polk St**
	Love's Travel Stop
410	**Bankhead Hwy**
	Love's Travel Stop
277	**FM 707 / Tye**
	Flying J Travel Plaza
42	**US 285 / Pecos**
	Flying J Travel Plaza

Interstate 27

I-27 runs north to south for 124 miles from Amarillo to Lubbock. Northbound travelers should read up the chart. Southbound travelers read down the chart.

Exit(mm)	Description
14	**FM 1729**
	New Deal Truck Stop

Interstate 30

Interstate 30 runs east to west for 224 miles from the Arkansas state line to I-20, west of Fort Worth. Eastbound travelers should read up the chart. Westbound travelers read down the chart.

Exit(mm)	Description
70	**FM 549**
	Love's Travel Stop

Interstate 35

Interstate 35 runs north to south for 504 miles from the Oklahoma state line to Laredo. I-35 splits into I-35E and I-35W near Hillsboro and comes together again in Denton. Northbound travelers should read up the chart. Southbound travelers read down the chart.

Exit(mm)	Description
496b	**W California St / Gainesville**
	Leonard Park (city park) west of exit, donations accepted. Park also has campsites with full hookups.
368a	**TX 22 / TX 171 / to Whitney**
	Love's Travel Stop
331	**New Rd**
	Flying J Travel Plaza
328	**FM 2063 / FM 2113 / Moody**
	Pilot Travel Center
193	**Conrads Rd / Kohlenberg Rd**
	Rip Griffin Travel Center
(180)	Rest Area
144	**Fischer Rd**
	Love's Travel Stop

Interstate 35W

Interstate 35W runs north to south for 85 miles. It splits from I-35 near Hillsboro and rejoins I-35 in Denton. Northbound travelers should read up the chart. Southbound travelers read down the chart.

Exit(mm)	Description
65	**TX 170**
	Pilot Travel Center
40	**Garden Acres Dr**
	Love's Travel Stop

Interstate 37

I-37 runs north to south for 143 miles from I-35 in San Antonio to Corpus Christi. Northbound travelers should read up the chart. Southbound travelers read down the chart.

Exit(mm)	Description
3a	**Navigation Blvd**
	Corpus Christi Truck Stop

Interstate 40

Interstate 40 runs east to west for 177 miles from the Oklahoma state line to the New Mexico state line. Eastbound travelers should read up the chart. Westbound travelers read down the chart.

Exit(mm)	Description
76	**TX 468 Spur / to Airport**
	Flying J Travel Plaza
75	**TX 335 Loop / Lakeside Rd**
	Pilot Travel Center
74	**Whitaker Rd**
	Love's Travel Stop
	TA Travel Center
36	**US 385 / Vega**
	Texas Quick Stop

Interstate 45

Interstate 45 runs north to south for about 286 miles from Dallas to TX Highway 87 in Galveston. Northbound travelers should read up the chart. Southbound travelers read down the chart.

Exit(mm)	Description
238	**FM 1603**
	Corner Food Mart
198	**FM 27 / to Wortham**
	Love's Travel Stop
64	**Richey Rd**
	Flying J Travel Plaza
1c	**Teichman Rd / Galveston**
	Harborside Food Mart

Other Locations

City or Town	Description
Bishop	Circle K at 201 US 77
Borger	Huber Park (city) located at south end of Main St at Pine St, free, easy access and ample turn-around space. RV parking spaces also available, sites are back in and paved with water and electric hookups.

Breckenridge	City park on E Walker St (US 180)
Corpus Christi	Padre Island National Seashore. Follow S Padre Island Dr from town. The dump station and water fill are at the entrance of the campground, which is near the visitor center. Must pay entrance fee of $10 before entering.
Decatur	Allsup's at 1305 US 287
Del Rio	Del Rio Civic Center at 1915 Veterans Blvd (US 90). Located in the back of the parking lot. Has water connection. Easy to get in and out of.
Del Rio	Diablo East Marina, approximately 8 miles west of Del Rio off US 90. Site provided free of charge by the National Park Service.
Dumas	Texhoma Park (city park) on US 87 west end of town. The city provides free overnight camping spaces with electricity at each site. There is also a free (donation accepted) dump station and water at the south end of park.
Eagle Pass	Valley Mart on US 277
Edinburg	Love's Travel Stop northbound US 281 at exit for FM 2812, 956-316-1782
Edna	Love's Travel Stop at US 59 and Milby Road
Frisco	Hidden Cove City Park west of Frisco on Hackberry Creek Park Rd (no fee if camping, $5 if not)
Gilmer	RV park at the Yamboree grounds on US 271 north of town
Graham	Fireman's City Park on TX 67. Also has 28 RV sites with hookups.
Graham	Lake Eddelman City Park on US 380. Also has 12 RV sites with hookups.
Hawkins	Lake Hawkins RV Park (county park), 903-769-4545, $2. Go west 3 miles on US 80 and one mile north on Hwy 3440.
Iowa Park	Rest Areas on US 287 (Northwest Freeway), both directions of travel, no fee, northwest of Wichita Falls
Jacksonville	Lake Jacksonville Recreation Area about 3 miles southwest of town
Lamesa	City park on US 180, free. Also has 8 campsites with hookups for Rvers.
Lampasas	Public dump station in city park on US 281, no fee
Lubbock	Chisum Travel Center, one mile outside Loop 289 on US 84, free
Lufkin	Love's Travel Stop at TX 287 and Ford Chapel Rd (FM 841)

Mason	Mason city park one mile south of town square. Turn into city park/golf course from US 87; at first intersection amid golf course, take 45 degree angle left turn into second group of RV sites; dump is on left. Can handle all size rigs. Several budget RV sites available in park with water, electric and sewer.
Mineola	Civic Center at 1150 N Newsom St one block east of US 69
Odem	Odem Truck Stop at 1206 US 77
Perryton	Wigham city park on Main St (US 83) between SE 9th Ave and SE 11th Ave, RV sites with hookups available
Quitman	Jim Hogg City Park just south of Wood County Courthouse on TX 37
Shepherd	Champion Travel Plaza at US 59 and FM 2914
Stephenville	City park just off the downtown square on Graham St (TX 108), 1/2 mile north of US 67/US 377 S Loop
Waller	Love's Travel Stop at US 290 and FM 2920
Wichita Falls	City of Wichita Falls RV park near Texas Travel Information Center, no charge
Winnsboro	City park on Hope Ln near junction of FM 515 (E Coke Rd) and FM 852 (Gilmer Rd).

Utah

Below is a list of RV dump stations in Utah. Listed first are those easily accessed from Interstate highways followed by those in other locations throughout the state.

Interstate 15

Interstate 15 runs north to south for about 403 miles from the Idaho state line to the Arizona state line. Parts are shared with I-80 and I-84. Northbound travelers should read up the chart. Southbound travelers read down the chart.

Exit(mm)	Description
364	**US 91 / Brigham City**
	Flying J Travel Plaza
360	**UT 315 / to Willard**
	Flying J Travel Plaza
346	**UT 104 / 21st St / Ogden**
	Flying J Travel Plaza
320	**UT 68 / Bountiful / Woods Cross**
	RB's One Stop
308	**UT 201 / 21st St / 13th St**
	Flying J Travel Plaza
254	**UT 115 / Payson**
	Flying J Travel Plaza, 840 N Main, 801-465-9281, free
222	**UT 28 / Nephi**
	Circle C Car & Truck Plaza
	Flying J Travel Plaza
	Tri-Mart Fuel Stop
78	**UT 141 / Parowan**
	TA Travel Center
8	**Saint George Blvd**
	Premium Oil

Interstate 70

Interstate 70 runs east to west for 232 miles from the Colorado state line to I-15 exit 132 near Beaver. Eastbound travelers should read up the chart. Westbound travelers read down the chart.

Exit(mm)	Description
162	**UT 19 / Green River**
	West Winds Truck Stop
158	**UT 19 / Green River**
	West Winds Truck Stop
40	**Main St / Richfield**
	Flying J Travel Plaza

Interstate 80

Interstate 80 runs east to west for 197 miles from the Wyoming state line to the Nevada state line. Part of it is also I-15. Eastbound travelers should read up the chart. Westbound travelers read down the chart.

Exit(mm)	Description
164	**Coalville**
	Holiday Hills
308	**UT 201 / 21st St / 13th St**
	Flying J Travel Plaza
99	**UT 36 / to Tooele**
	Flying J Travel Plaza
	TA Travel Center

Interstate 84

Interstate 84 runs east to west for about 120 miles from I-80 near Coalville to the Idaho state line. Portions are shared with I-15. Eastbound travelers should read up the chart. Westbound travelers read down the chart.

Exit(mm)	Description
346	**UT 104 / 21st St / Ogden**
	Flying J Travel Plaza

360	**UT 315 / to Willard**
	Flying J Travel Plaza
364	**US 91 / Brigham City**
	Flying J Travel Plaza
40	**UT 102 / Tremonton / Bothwell**
	Golden Spike Travel Plaza
7	**Snowville**
	Flying J Travel Plaza

Interstate 215

Interstate 215 is 29 miles long. It forms a partial loop around Salt Lake City. Exit numbers increase in a clockwise direction.

Exit(mm)	Description
18	**UT 171 / West Valley City**
	State Trailer Supply
	Comments: From exit, go east on UT 171 to Redwood Rd and turn south. No fee. This is a very large RV supply store with several large repair and installation bays.
28	**UT 68 / Redwood Rd**
	Flying J Travel Plaza

Other Locations

City or Town	Description
Duchesne	Gateway 66, 655 W Main St (US 40)
Jensen	Dinosaur Gifts & Souvenirs, $3. Located at the store just outside Dinosaur National Monument (Quarry entrance). Fee waived with store purchase. Closed in winter.
Kanab	Samco on US 89/89A at 289 S 100 E
Logan	Logan fairgrounds, west of US 89 near intersection of W 500 S and S 500 W, free. On west side of fairgrounds, just north of Armory.
Moab	Quality RV Service & Supply, 850 S US 191, $4 fee, on west side of street 1/2 block south of McDonald's, 24-hour access, pay on honor system after business hours, potable water available
Price	Public dump station at fairgrounds. Take Exit 240 on US 6 at UT 55 / W 100 N and follow signs uphill to fairgrounds.
Saint George	Premium Oil at 181 UT 18 just north of UT 34

Vermont

Below is a list of RV dump stations in Vermont. Listed first are those easily accessed from Interstate highways followed by those in other locations throughout the state.

Interstate 89

Interstate 89 in Vermont runs north to south for 130 miles from the United States/Canada border to the New Hampshire state line. Exit numbers are based on the consecutive numbering system. Northbound travelers should read up the chart. Southbound travelers read down the chart.

Exit(mm)	Description
14e	**US 2 / Williston Rd / Burlington**
	Pete's RV Center, 4015 Williston Rd, 802-864-9350, free. RV dealer is east of exit near the airport. Enter left of building. Dump station is at rear, complete drive around. Daylight hours only.

Other Locations

City or Town	Description
Jeffersonville	Madonna Mobil on VT 15 in town, $7.50
Rutland	Wastewater treatment plant at West St (US 4 Bus) and Green Hill Ln, free.

Virginia

Below is a list of RV dump stations in Virginia. Listed first are those easily accessed from Interstate highways followed by those in other locations throughout the state.

Interstate 64

Interstate 64 runs east to west for 299 miles from I-264 in Chesapeake to the West Virginia state line. Part of it is shared with I-81. Eastbound travelers should read up the chart. Westbound travelers read down the chart.

Exit(mm)	Description
250b	**VA 105 / Fort Eustis Blvd / Newport News** Newport News City Park campground at 13564 Jefferson Ave, $3 fee if not camping, free if camping
195	**US 11 / Lee Highway** Lee Hi Travel Plaza

Interstate 77

Interstate 77 runs north to south for 67 miles from the West Virginia state line to the North Carolina state line. Part of it is also I-81. Northbound travelers should read up the chart. Southbound travelers read down the chart.

Exit(mm)	Description
41	**VA 610 / Peppers Ferry / Wytheville** TA Travel Center
77	**Service Rd** Flying J Travel Plaza

Interstate 81

I-81 runs north to south for 325 miles from the West Virginia state line to the Tennessee state line. Portions are shared with I-64 and I-77.

Northbound travelers should read up the chart. Southbound travelers read down the chart.

Exit(mm)	Description
323	**VA 669**
	Flying J Travel Plaza
195	**US 11 / Lee Highway**
	Lee Hi Travel Plaza
84	**VA 619 / to Grahams Forge**
	Love's Travel Stop
77	**Service Rd**
	Flying J Travel Plaza
72	**I-77 N**
	TA Travel Center
67	**US 11 (nb access only)**
	Wilco Travel Plaza

Interstate 95

Interstate 95 runs north to south for 179 miles from the Maryland state line to the North Carolina state line. Northbound travelers should read up the chart. Southbound travelers read down the chart.

Exit(mm)	Description
152	**VA 234 / Dumfries**
	Prince William Trailer Village, 2.5 miles west of exit on VA 234, $5. Clean facilities at the trailer park. Easy access, non-potable water hose available.
104	**VA 207 / to Bowling Green**
	Flying J Travel Plaza
98	**VA 30 / Doswell**
	Doswell All American Plaza
89	**VA 802**
	TA Travel Center
11b	**US 58 / Emporia**
	Public dump station is in the corner of lot for Burger King/Citgo station on US 58, no fee.
4	**Moores Ferry Rd / to Skippers**
	Love's Travel Stop, free

Other Locations

City or Town	Description
Centreville	Bull Run Regional Park off US 29, 703-631-0550, $21
Reston	Lake Fairfax County Park campground off VA 606, no charge
Virginia Beach	Dam Neck Navy Base (military ID required to gain access), no fee. Base has a small RV campground; dump is up the road from there. Water available and coin-op washing area to wash your RV.

Washington

Below is a list of RV dump stations in Washington. Listed first are those easily accessed from Interstate highways followed by those in other locations throughout the state.

Interstate 5

I-5 runs north to south for 277 miles from the United States/Canada border to the Oregon state line. Northbound travelers should read up the chart. Southbound travelers read down the chart.

Exit(mm)	Description
258	**Bakerview Rd**
	Yorky's Exxon - free with fuel purchase, $4 without
256a	**WA 539 / Meridian St**
	Meridian Shell - dump station located behind car wash, limited to RVs up to 32 feet long
254	**Iowa St / State St**
	Iowa Street Chevron - free with fuel purchase, $3 without
232	**Cook Rd / Sedro-Woolley**
	Cook Road Texaco
227	**College Way / Mount Vernon**
	Lions Park at 501 Freeway Dr
(207)	Rest Area
(188)	Rest Area (sb)
176	**N 175th St / Richmond Highlands**
	Evergreen RV Supply, 16610 Aurora Ave N, 206-542-1181, $3. Go west at exit and then south on Aurora Ave.
(141)	Rest Area (nb)
99	**WA 121 / 93rd Ave SW**
	Shell truck stop just west of exit, $10
(12)	Rest Area (sb)
(11)	Rest Area (nb)

Interstate 82

Interstate 82 runs east to west for 133 miles from the Oregon state line to I-90 exit 110 near Ellensburg. Eastbound travelers should read up the chart. Westbound travelers read down the chart.

Exit(mm)	Description
80	**Gap Rd** Rest Area Horse Heaven Hills Travel Plaza
54	**Yakima Valley Highway / Zillah** City-maintained dump station is on First Ave across from supermarket on west end of town, donation requested
52	**Meyers Rd / Zillah** City-maintained dump station is on First Ave across from supermarket on west end of town, donation requested
(24)	Rest Area (eb)
(22)	Rest Area (wb)

Interstate 90

Interstate 90 runs east to west for about 300 miles from the Idaho state line to I-5 in Seattle. Eastbound travelers should read up the chart. Westbound travelers read down the chart.

Exit(mm)	Description
(242)	Rest Area (eb)
(199)	Rest Area (wb)
179	**WA 17** Husky Hillstop at 1253 Pioneer Way Moses Lake Exxon at 1725 Kittleson Rd
(162)	Rest Area (wb)
(161)	Rest Area (eb)
(89)	Rest Area
85	**Sunset Hwy / Cle Elum** Shell service station, free with fuel purchase
70	**Railroad St / Easton** Lake Easton State Park
17	**E Lake Sammamish Pkwy SE / Issaquah** Issaquah Village RV Park, 650 1st Ave NE, 800-258-9233, $5

15	WA 900 / Renton Rd / Issaquah
	Lake Sammamish State Park, $10 fee

Interstate 182

Interstate 182 runs east to west for about 14 miles from US 12 in Pasco to Interstate 82. Eastbound travelers should read up the chart. Westbound travelers read down the chart.

Exit(mm)	Description
5b	**George Washington Way / Richland** Columbia Point, no fee. From exit go north to first stop light and then east about one mile to city-owned boat launch.

Other Locations

City or Town	Description
Anacortes	Washington City Park west of WA 20
Anacortes	Wastewater treatment plant at 4th St and T Ave. From WA 20 follow R Ave to 4th St and turn right. No charge. Open weekdays 8:30am to 4:30 pm; 9am to 11am on holidays. Water fill station is nearby.
Bellevue	Chevron Station at intersection of Richards Rd and SE 32nd St. Not easily reached from Freeways. Local map recommended. Washdown water at dump. Back in, with guidance. $2.50 with fill-up, $5 without.
Bremerton	Wastewater treatment plant near intersection of WA 3 and Loxie Eagans Blvd, free, take frontage road on southwest side of intersection behind Ford dealership, open 7am to 2pm year-round
Burlington	Lions Club Park at WA 20 and N Regent St, $1 donation requested, fresh water available at site
Burlington	Rotary Park on S Section St south of E Rio Vista Ave
Chewelah	49er Motel & RV Park, 311 S Park St, $5 fee, south end of town on east side of US 395 (Park St)
Colfax	Palouse Empire Fairgrounds 5 miles west of Colfax on WA 26
Colville	Northeast Washington Fairgrounds on Astor Ave 3 blocks west of US 395
Colville	Whitty's Chevron at 370 W 5th Ave (US 395)

Coupeville	Waste treatment plant on NE Kinney St. From WA 20 and N Main St, go north to NE 9th St and turn east. Go east three blocks to NE Kinney St. There is no water to rinse with. Free
Elma	Gateway Exxon Truck Stop at US 12 Business and Main St
Elma	Rest area on WA 8 about two miles east of town. Free
Enumclaw	Jerry's Chevron Station at corner of Blake St and Griffin Ave (WA 410), 360-825-7707. $3 fee without fill-up, $1.50 with fill-up.
Fairholm	Public campground in Olympic National Park at west end of Lake Crescent off US 101. $3 fee.
Friday Harbor	Wastewater treatment plant at intersection of Tucker Ave and Harbor St about 1/2 mile from ferry landing, no fee
Hatton	Hatton Coulee Rest Area at US 395 and WA 26 interchange; fee unknown
Joyce	Salt Creek Recreation Area (county park) off WA 112 about 4 miles northeast of town
Kennewick	Tesoro gas station at US 395 and 7th St, $5. The dump is in back.
Leavenworth	Nason Creek Campground (USFS) on US 2 about 4 miles west of Lake Wenatchee cutoff
Leavenworth	Nason Creek Rest Area along US 2 on north side of highway about three miles west of Coles Corner. Free
Lynden	Berthusen City Park at 8837 Berthusen Rd about three miles northwest of Lynden
Lynden	Cenex/Whatcom Farmers Co-op at corner of Main St and 3rd St, $2
Maple Falls	Silver Lake County Park - free to park guests, $5 for non-guests
Marysville	Public Works Dept at 1st St and Columbia Ave
Monroe	On US 2 (also WA 2) next to Sky Valley Traders store, $5 fee, pay inside store
Moses Lake	Lakeside Conoco at 208 E Broadway
Oak Harbor	Deception Pass State Park north of town, $5
Oak Harbor	Oak Harbor Beach Park (city park) near the junction of WA 20 and SE Pioneer Way. $3 fee.
Ocean Shores	A dump station is located next to the public works building on Point Brown Ave
Okanogan	Flying B at 2042 Elmway (US 97A, WA 20)
Omak	Eastside Park on Omak Ave
Omak	Omak Chevron at 30 S Main St
Omak	Omak Texaco Food Mart at US 97 and E Riverside

Port Angeles	Clallam County Fair Grounds at 1608 W 16th St
Port Angeles	Road Runner Food Mart / 76 Station at 1023 E Front St
Port Orchard	Union 76 Station at WA 16 and Sedgwick Rd; located on the north side of the car wash; free
Pullman	City sewage plant on Park St, no fee, follow signs from WA 270
Raymond	Raymond RV & Marine, 1875 Ocean Ave, 360-942-2906, $5 fee. On US 101 about 1/2 mile west of town. Very easy to enter and exit. 12 RV sites on the Willapa River.
Republic	Slagle City Park at N Kean St and W 6th St (WA 20)
Sequim	Chevron Station in town at east end of Washington St, next to Les Schwab Tires. $3 fee or free with fuel purchase.
Sequim	Dungeness Recreation Area (county park) on Lotzgesell Rd about 7 miles northwest of Sequim
Shelton	Mason County Fairgrounds at 751 W Fairgrounds Rd west of US 101
Spokane	Riverside State Park, 509-465-5064. Dump station is located just inside campground gate near "Bowl and Pitcher" area on the Spokane River.
Stanwood	Camano Island State Park about 14 miles southwest of town. Free if you are camping, otherwise the fee is $5.
Sumas	Sumas RV Park & Campground, 9600 Easterbrook, 360-988-8875, $5
Tonasket	Visitor Center at 215 S Whitcomb - also has 8 RV camping sites with hookups
Walla Walla	Cenex Convenience Store at 706 W Rose St
Walla Walla	Lyons Park (city park) on Larch St at SE 12th St; in parking lot of park; donations accepted
Wenatchee	Wenatchee Confluence State Park near US 2/97 and WA 285 junction in the Olds Station area, $5 fee.

West Virginia

Below is a list of RV dump stations in West Virginia. Listed first are those easily accessed from Interstate highways followed by those in other locations throughout the state.

Interstate 64

Interstate 64 runs east to west for 189 miles from the Virginia state line to the Kentucky state line. Portions are shared with I-77 and the West Virginia Turnpike. Eastbound travelers should read up the chart. Westbound travelers read down the chart.

Exit(mm)	Description
(72)	Turnpike Service Area (wb)
45	**Vankirk Dr / Beckley**
	Beckley Travel Plaza/Tamarack Crafts Center
(35)	Rest Area

Interstate 68

I-68 is 32 miles long. It runs east to west from the Maryland state line to I-79 Exit 148 near Morgantown. Eastbound travelers should read up the chart. Westbound travelers read down the chart.

Exit(mm)	Description
(31)	Welcome Center (wb)

Interstate 70

Interstate 70 runs east to west for 14 miles from the Pennsylvania state line to the Ohio state line. Eastbound travelers should read up the chart. Westbound travelers read down the chart.

Exit(mm)	Description
(13)	Welcome Center (wb)
11	**WV 41 / Dallas Pike**
	Dallas Pike Travel Express

Interstate 77

I-77 runs north to south for 187 miles from the Ohio state line to the Virginia state line. Portions are also I-64 and the West Virginia Turnpike. Northbound travelers should read up the chart. Southbound travelers read down the chart.

Exit(mm)	Description
(166)	Welcome Center (sb) / Rest Area (nb)
(72)	Turnpike Service Area (nb)
45	**Vankirk Dr / Beckley**
	Beckley Travel Plaza/Tamarack Crafts Center
(17)	Turnpike Service Area (nb)

Interstate 79

Interstate 79 runs north to south for 161 miles from the Pennsylvania state line to I-77 exit 104 near Charleston. Northbound travelers should read up the chart. Southbound travelers read down the chart.

Exit(mm)	Description
(159)	Welcome Center (sb)
(123)	Rest Area
(85)	Rest Area
(49)	Rest Area

Other Locations

City or Town	Description
New Martinsville	Public dump station on the corner of Main St and Harlan Dr near the public park/boat launch, no fee

Wisconsin

Below is a list of RV dump stations in Wisconsin. Listed first are those easily accessed from Interstate highways followed by those in other locations throughout the state.

Interstate 39

Interstate 39 is about 205 miles long. It runs north to south from US 51 in Merrill to the Illinois state line. Part of it is also shared with I-90 and I-94. Northbound travelers should read up the chart. Southbound travelers read down the chart.

Exit(mm)	Description
188	**Rib Mountain Dr / CR N**
	Rib Mountain Travel Center
132	**US 51 / to Madison**
	Token Creek Park (county park), $2 fee
	Wisconsin RV World

Interstate 43

Interstate 43 runs north to south for 192 miles from US 41 in Green Bay to I-90/I-39 in Beloit. Portions of it is shared with I-94 and I-894. Northbound travelers should read up the chart. Southbound travelers read down the chart.

Exit(mm)	Description
187	**East Shore Dr / N Webster Ave / Green Bay**
	Bay Beach City Park
157	**CR V / Hillcrest Rd / Francis Creek**
	Fun-N-Fast Travel Center

Interstate 90

Interstate 90 runs east to west for 188 miles from the Illinois state line to the Minnesota state line. Parts of it are shared with I-39 and I-94.

Eastbound travelers should read up the chart. Westbound travelers read down the chart.

Exit(mm)	Description
132	**US 51 / to Madison** Token Creek Park (county park), $2 fee Wisconsin RV World
69	**WI 82 / Mauston** Kwik Trip
61	**WI 80 / New Lisbon** New Lisbon Travel Center The Bunk House

Interstate 94

I-94 runs east to west for about 350 miles from the Illinois state line to the Minnesota state line. Portions are shared with I-39, I-43, and I-90. Eastbound travelers should read up the chart. Westbound travelers read down the chart.

Exit(mm)	Description
322	**WI 100 / W Ryan Rd / to Oak Creek** Flying J Travel Plaza
319	**W College Ave / Milwaukee** Prosser RV / Cruise America, 6146 S Howell Ave, 414-766-1079, $35 fee. Full-service dump (no do-it-yourself) by appointment only. From exit, go east to WI 38 (Howell Ave) and turn left (north); one block on east side of street.
306	**WI 181 / S 84th St** Wisconsin State Fair Park south of exit. Dump station is beside campground and has plenty of turnaround space. $7
132	**US 51 / to Madison** Token Creek Park (county park), $2 fee Wisconsin RV World
69	**WI 82 / Mauston** Kwik Trip
61	**WI 80 / New Lisbon** New Lisbon Travel Center The Bunk House

143	**US 12 / WI 21 / Tomah** Kwik Trip, dump is located behind main building next to small out building.
116	**WI 54** Black River Crossing Oasis Flying J Travel Plaza

Other Locations

City or Town	Description
Abbotsford	Shell Travel Center on west side of town off WI 29, no fee. Huge lot with lots of space for pulling and turning around.
Antigo	Antigo Lake Park (city park) in downtown Antigo; east of US 45; rinse water available; camping.
Baileys Harbor	Baileys Grove Travel Park & Campground, 2552 CR F, $10
Baraboo	BP station on WI 33 about three miles east of US 12, $5
Baraboo	Devil's Lake State Park, free but a daily or seasonal park sticker is required for entrance to park. From US 12 travel east on Hwy 159 1/2 mile to Hwy 123. Turn right and follow to main entrance to park. Follow curve in road to left before entering park and proceed down the hill. Turn onto first road to the right, which is actually an entrance to one of the campground, and follow circle all the way around going right. Dump station will be on your right side when you have almost completely circled back to the entrance you came in at.
Baraboo	Wastewater treatment plant off WI 113, free. Go south from Circus World museum to Manchester St and turn right. Plant is 1/4 mile on your left.
Beaver Dam	Derge County Park about 7 miles northwest of town via County Road G and County Road CP
Boulder Junction	North Trout Lake Campground (Northern Highland State Forest), no fee. Campground is about six miles off US 51 via CR M or three miles south of town. Turn left at campground and then first right and follow to dump station.
Cadott	River Country Plaza at WI 27 and WI 29
Chippewa Falls	Wastewater treatment plant, 1125 W River St (WI 29), 715-726-2745, free, across from River Country Co-op
Colby	Super 29 Shell at 1210 WI 13
Columbus	Astico County Park at WI 16/60 and CR TT about 3 miles east of Columbus

Eagle River	Wastewater treatment plant on W Division St, west of US 45, $5 fee. Very large area to turn around. Rinse water available. Open 24/7
Elkhart Lake	Sheboygan Marsh County Park about 2 miles west of town, $4 fee
Fond du Lac	County fairgrounds at E 17th St and Martin Ave, no fee. The dump that was for non-campers was removed; you must back into a site and dump at a site.
Granton	Beckers BP Highway Service on US 10 between Marshfield and Neillsville, no fee. Sells diesel as well as gas. Also has a convenience store.
Green Bay	Van Boxtel RV Center at 1956 Bond St, no fee. From US 41, take the WI 29/Shawano Ave exit, east to N Taylor St, north to Bond St.
Marshfield	Central Wisconsin State Fairgrounds at S Vine Ave and E 17th St
Minocqua	Lakeland Sanitary District at 8780 Morgan Rd about 2 1/2 miles northwest of town via US 51 and WI 70
Minong	Link Stop convenience store and A&W on US 53 behind the store by the LP tank. Open year-round, free, rinse water available, no rinse hose.
Oconto	Holtwood Park (city park) west of US 41, $2. Turn west at the south end of Oconto River Bridge and go about four blocks; turn right to campground; dump on right side of road.
Oshkosh	BP-Oshkosh Plaza on Green Valley Rd at US 41 and WI 76, $5 fee, 920-233-1165
Park Falls	City of Park Falls Public Works Department on Case Ave about 1/4 mile south of WI 182. Free.
Platteville	City Garage on Valley Road off US 151
Reedsburg	BP/Amoco at WI 33 and CR H, no fee
Rhinelander	Wastewater treatment plant on Boyce Dr about 1/4 mile south of Kemp St; free for residents, $3 for others
Rice Lake	Cenex service station of US 53 Exit 143, 715-736-0800. Free. Dump station is in back of the store.
Richland Center	City wastewater treatment plant on S Orange St west of US 14, no fee. Dump station accessible from US 14 between intersections of Seminary St and southbound WI 80. City posted a small red "RV Dump Station" sign. Limited turnaround for big rigs or rigs towing vehicles.
River Falls	Hoffman Park one block west of WI 35 off Division St (CR M), $2

Sauk City	Cenex station at 740 Phillips Blvd (US 12), $3 fee, free with fill-up.
Shawano	Shawano County Fairgrounds at 990 E Green Bay St in town
Shawano	Shawano County Park at W5785 Lake Dr, about 5 miles northeast of town via WI 47 and CR H
Siren	Holiday gas station, 24096 State Road 35 (2nd Ave), 715-349-2410, fee unknown
Superior	BP gas station southeast end of town on the northeast side of US 2. Easy access. Free with gas purchase, $5 without. They also have potable and non-potable water available.
Tomah	Public dump station at Fort McCoy on WI 21. The dump is free to the public but you will need to show a picture ID when going through the gate.
Tomahawk	Public dump station behind city garage on US 51 Bus, three blocks west of Higly's Propane & Appliance store in downtown Tomahawk, no fee.
Washburn	Memorial Park (city park) off WI 13 at 6th Ave E, north end of town. Fee unkown.
Wisconsin Rapids	City wastewater treatment plant at 2540 1st St S (east of Riverview Expy Bridge), $1 fee, non-potable water for flushing tanks available as is potable water for freshwater tank

Wyoming

Below is a list of RV dump stations in Wyoming. Listed first are those easily accessed from Interstate highways followed by those in other locations throughout the state.

Interstate 25

Interstate 25 runs north to south for 300 miles from I-90 in Buffalo to the Colorado state line. Northbound travelers should read up the chart. Southbound travelers read down the chart.

Exit(mm)	Description
299	**US 16 / Buffalo**
	Big Horn Travel Plaza, 207 S Bypass Rd, 307-684-5246, $3 fee
	Cenex Truck Stop, 501 E Hart St, 307-684-9513, free
185	**WY 258 / Wyoming Blvd / Casper**
	Flying J Travel Plaza, 41 SE Wyoming Blvd, 307-473-1750
182	**WY 253 / Brooks Rd / Hat Six Rd**
	Eastgate Travel Plaza
126	**US 18 / US 20 / Orin**
	Rest Area
	Orin Junction Truck Stop
(54)	Rest Area
7	**WY 212 / College Dr**
	Welcome Center
	Flying J Travel Plaza, 2250 Etchepare Dr, 307-635-2918, free
	Love's Travel Stop, 3305 W College Dr, 307-632-2444, free

Interstate 80

Interstate 80 runs east to west for about 403 miles from the Nebraska state line to the Utah state line. Eastbound travelers should read up the chart. Westbound travelers read down the chart.

Exit(mm)	Description
370	**US 30 / Archer**
	Sapp Brothers Truck Stop, 3350 I-80 Service Rd, 307-632-6600, $5 fee

311	**WY 130 / WY 230 / Snowy Range Rd / Laramie**
	High Country Sportsman
214	**Higley Blvd / Rawlins**
	Rip Griffin Travel Center
209	**Johnson Rd**
	Flying J Travel Plaza
173	**Wamsutter**
	Sinclair Fuel Stop
	Wamsutter Conoco Service
104	**US 191 / Elk St / Rock Springs**
	Flying J Travel Plaza, 650 Stagecoach Dr, 307-362-4231, free
68	**Little America**
	Little America Truck Stop
(6)	Welcome Center

Interstate 90

Interstate 90 runs east to west for 208 miles from the South Dakota state line to the Montana state line. Eastbound travelers should read up the chart. Westbound travelers read down the chart.

Exit(mm)	Description
126	**WY 59 / Gillette**
	Dalbey Memorial Park one mile south of exit off WY 59
	Flying J Travel Plaza, 1810 Douglas Hwy, 307-682-3562, free
25	**US 14 / WY 334 / Sheridan**
	Holiday Gas Station, south of exit, 936 E Brundage Ln, 307-672-8729, free
	Comments: Dump station is located on the southwest corner of the gas station and is best accessed by smaller RVs. May be closed in winter.
	Washington City Park, on Coffeen Ave
	Comments: From I-90 exit proceed west to first traffic light and turn right. Proceed about one mile and cross Little Goose Creek bridge. Park is about 1/4 mile beyond the bridge on the right.
23	**WY 330 / 5th St / Sheridan**
	Visitor Information Center, closed in winter

Other Locations

City or Town	Description
Afton	City of Afton information center, free
Alpine	Nordic Market at US 89 and US 26
Basin	Overland Express Mart, 155 N 4th St, 307-568-2722, free
Basin	Washington Park (city park), open May thru Sep, 307-568-3331, free
Buffalo	Bighorn National Forest public dump station on US 16 about three miles west of Powder River Pass, on south side of highway, fresh water available, donation
Casper	Bentz's Town Pump, 701 W Collins Dr, 307-234-1435, $2.50 fee for standard RVs. Also offers a portable dump catch basin for buses, $10 fee.
Casper	Rest Area on WY 220 adjacent to Independence Rock on the Oregon Trail about 53 miles southwest of Casper
Cody	City of Cody dump station located 1/2 mile east of Cody, next to the Wyoming Vietnam Memorial Park, on the north side of highway.
Cokeville	Flying J Travel Plaza at US 30 and WY 232
Green River	Wastewater treatment plant on E Astle Ave, free
Jackson	Reynolds Petroleum, 1055 W Broadway, free with fill-up, without fill-up a fee of $5 to $25 is charged depending on size of RV
Jackson	Wrangler Petroleum, 580 W Broadway, also has propane, dump available in summer only
Lander	Popo Agie One Stop at 8116 E Main St (US 287)
Lovell	City park at E 2nd St and Quebec Ave
Mountain View	Bullock's Fuels, 650 N Hwy 414, 307-782-6324, $2 fee
Pinedale	Warren Bridge Campground (Bureau of Land Management) about 20 miles northwest of town via US 191. $3
Riverton	Bob's Hilltop Sinclair, 912 W Main St, 307-856-1412, $2 fee
Riverton	C-Plus Conoco, 203 N Federal Blvd (US 26), 307-856-1100
Riverton	Wind River RV Park, 1618 E Park Ave, 800-528-3913, fee unknown. RV Park is 6 blocks east of US 26.
Shoshoni	Trail Town Supply at US 20 and US 26
Thermopolis	Texaco Southside Travel Center at 167 US 20
Torrington	Torrington Travel Terminal at 1500 US 26
Wright	Rest area on WY 387, just west of WY 59

Appendix A

How to Empty Holding Tanks

Here's a suggestion on how to empty your RV's holding tanks.

First of all, don't open any valves until the proper time! Doing so will be met with rather unpleasant results. You may consider wearing a pair of rubber gloves in the event some effluent gets on your hands. Some folks will also wear rubber boots. As long as you're careful, any splashing is minimal.

Remove the holding tank outlet cap and connect your three-inch sewer hose to the outlet of your holding tank. Extend the hose to the opening of the dump station, which is usually a hole in the ground that is slightly larger than the three-inch hose.

Insert your sewer hose into the dump station's hole about four to six inches. Use the hole's cover, a brick, or something heavy enough to hold the sewer hose in place so it doesn't come out of the hole.

Once you're sure that all is connected and held down, open your black tank valve. You'll hear the effluent flow and eventually it'll slow, then stop. Close the black tank valve.

Now open the gray tank valve. Again, you'll hear water flow, then slow, and stop. Close the gray tank valve.

At this point, you're almost done. If you want to flush and rinse your tanks once more, you can do so by filling your tanks to two-thirds full and repeat the emptying process. If others are waiting to use the dump station, skip this step.

Recheck that both your black and gray water tank valves are closed and disconnect the sewer hose from your tank outlet. Replace the tank outlet cover. Lift the end of the sewer hose (the end you just disconnected) to completely drain the hose into the dump station. If a non-potable water hose is available, run water through the sewer hose to rinse it out. Remove the sewer hose from the dump station hole and rinse the outside of the hose. Rinse the area around the hole to ensure that any spillage has been cleaned up and cover the dump station hole.

Go in to your RV and add about five gallons of water (about three flushes) to your black tank and then add the appropriate amount of holding tank treatment. If you use a treatment for your gray tank, do that as well.

The task of emptying your RV's holding tanks is finished! Now it's time to move on to your next destination.

Appendix B

Dump Station Tips

Here are some tips to follow when emptying your RV's holding tanks.

- Don't dump the black-water tank until it is at least two-thirds full. Don't leave the black-water tank valve open when hooked up at a campsite. This will cause liquids to drain, leaving solid waste behind to harden on the bottom of the tank.

- Use a heavy-duty sewer hose about 6 to 8 feet long to make handling easier.

- Carry an extra garden hose for rinsing in case the dump station doesn't have one. Store this in an area where it won't come into contact with your drinking water hose.

- Never use your fresh water hose for rinsing sewer hoses or the dump station area.

- Wear protective rubber gloves and avoid touching the outside of the gloves.

- If others are waiting to use the dump station, skip the tank flushing and hose rinsing steps. Pull away from the dump station and then add some water and chemicals to the holding tanks.

- Never put anything other than the contents of your holding tanks into the dump station.

- Leave the dump station area cleaner than you found it.

Appendix C

Dump Station Abuse

For years RVers have been pulling into Interstate rest areas and other areas with free dump stations to empty their holding tanks. But because of abuse, many states are removing dump stations from their rest areas and campground owners and others view their dump stations as an expensive maintenance headache. Dump station abuse amounts to folks leaving a mess or putting things into the dump drain that just don't belong there. Remember, somebody has to clean up the mess or clean out the drain. Dump station abuse causes aggravation, creates a health hazard, and costs money. You can do your part to ensure RVers will continue to have free and clean dump stations by following the simple tips mentioned in Appendix B.

Appendix D

Interstate Cross Reference